HANOI HILTON

HOA LO PRISON

D1545180

8

9 (MAYO)

CELL BLOCK O

1

MEDIC SHACK

BATH AREA

QUIZ ROOMS

2

4

3

CAMP UNITY AREA

IN THE PRESENCE OF MINE ENEMIES
1965-1973

IN THE PRESENCE OF MINE ENEMIES

1965-1973

A PRISONER OF WAR

HOWARD AND PHYLLIS RUTLEDGE
WITH
MEL AND LYLA WHITE

Illustrations by Gerald Coffee

FLEMING H. REVELL COMPANY
Old Tappan, New Jersey

Scripture quotations in this volume are from the King James Version of the Bible.

Library of Congress Cataloging in Publication Data

Rutledge, Howard.
    In the presence of mine enemies, 1965-1973.

    1. Vietnamese Conflict, 1961-   --Prisoners
and prisons, North Vietnamese. 2. Vietnamese
Conflict, 1961-   --Personal narratives, American.
3. Rutledge, Howard. 4. Prisoners of war--
Religious life. I. Rutledge, Phyllis. II. White,
Mel. III. White, Lyla. IV. Title.
DS557.A675R87   959.704'37   73-7986
ISBN 0-8007-0624-2   5-15-75

To all who never stopped hoping and praying for
our return, and to God who answered those prayers.

Contents

Illustrations are by Gerald Coffee,
who was also a prisoner of war
in the "Hanoi Hilton."

Part I
Captain Howard E. Rutledge
1965-1973
Prisoner of War

1

Shot Down and Captured

My freedom ended November 28, 1965. I was the Executive Officer of Fighter Squadron 191 aboard the attack Carrier USS *Bon Homme Richard* in the Gulf of Tonkin. We were conducting round-the-clock missions over North Vietnam. This day I was a flight leader in a large force of fighter and attack aircraft. Our mission was to destroy a strategic bridge just northwest of Thanh Hoa. My F-8 Crusader jet, armed with two 2,000 lb. bombs, two air-to-air missiles, and four 20mm cannons, had catapulted from the carrier, rendezvoused with the squadron, refueled in the air, and approached the target as planned.

As I crossed from the safety of the sea to the enemy beaches, I signaled FEET DRY to the pilots of my flight and reported the overcast weather conditions to the strike leader. At almost 600 mph I broke through the haze at 5,000 feet and off to my right got a clear view of our target.

We suspected the area might be heavily protected and immediately I faced a fierce barrage of antiaircraft fire. I could see the guns below belching flame and knew that shells were exploding all around me; but after over 200 safe missions over Korea and North and South Vietnam, the thought of being hit never crossed my mind.

As I approached the roll-in point for my drop, two antiaircraft shells exploded somewhere in the tail section behind me. The pilot of a Crusader fighter sits right in the nose and cannot really see the fuselage aft. Because the plane responded satisfactorily and because I would be headed toward the safety of the sea at the end of the bombing run, I selected my afterburner and continued my attack on the target almost at the speed of sound. I dropped my bombs, and, still accelerating, turned to a heading toward the sea.

It was then my fighter received another hit. This time I knew it was a mortal blow. The plane pitched down about 20° and commenced an uncontrollable roll to the left.

I heard my wingman on the radio, "They are really shooting in here!"

I tried a quick transmission in reply, "I am hit! I am hit and bailing out!"

The plane was traveling like lightning and rolling uncontrollably. The stick went dead in my hands. The horizon spun past. We rolled 360°, and a few degrees before top-dead center I jerked at the ejection curtain. My escape seat hurled into the air as another shell burst under the cockpit itself. A fragment tore into my leg. I made one 360° tumble and saw the horizon pass. The chute deployed automatically, and I watched with horror as my plane exploded into a ball of flame before me.

"Thank You, God!" I prayed for the first time in twenty years, dangling 1,000 feet above North Vietnam. It was a short prayer of thanks. If I had waited another second to eject, I would have died in that explosion of bombs, jet fuel, and cannon shells. My grateful reveries were interrupted by a new danger.

Remember how bullets zing past the good guys in B-grade television westerns and old war movies? I could hear bullets singing past me and could see the holes they were making in my parachute. Instinctively, I hung limp in the shrouds to make the enemy believe I had been mortally wounded. Still curious

I watched with horror as my plane exploded into a ball of flame before me.

to see who could be firing, I cracked open my eyes, slowly turned my head downwards and, to my horror, discovered I was descending rapidly into the town square of a rather large village. A crowd was gathering. Everyone was gesturing in my direction, and I could hear them shouting excitedly.

Resurrected by the sight, I reached up and pulled the two front risers that altered my course and sent me drifting faster toward the flooded rice fields at the edge of town, and away from the welcoming committee that was forming there.

I had never parachuted from a plane before that day, and though it all seemed terribly unreal, I was functioning on instinct carefully trained into me by the U.S. Navy survival schools. In the last few seconds of descent, I could see that I was going to land about twenty yards to the north of a huge dike that ran east and west to the sea. For a navy pilot, the sea is friendly. I was hoping that those big, beautiful, search-and-rescue helicopters had been notified of my plight and were on their way to lift me back to safety. I had seen my wingman, Lt. Ken Masat, risk his own life to circle through the antiaircraft fire to check out my chute and get a sighting on my descent. He would notify them. If I could just stay free long enough to reach the dike and run for the sea, they would find me. But already I could count perhaps fifty men running in my direction. I landed standing up. Fortunately, I was knee-deep in mud; without that my legs would have broken almost certainly. Instinctively, I released my lower rocket fittings to get rid of the raft and survival paraphernalia. One release rocket wouldn't fire, and I struggled desperately to free myself.

By now I could hear voices shouting from all sides. In the two minutes it took to break free, only one young Vietnamese militiaman had gotten between me and that important dike. He was in his early twenties and carried a machete which he waved threateningly. Yelling at the top of his voice, he ran toward me, blocking my escape to the sea.

I jerked my 38 revolver from my survival gear, pulled back the hammer and pointed it at his chest, hoping to frighten him away. He didn't waver. Still screaming and wielding the machete high over his head, he ran to point-blank range. I pulled the trigger, and he fell dead at my feet. I will never forget the look on his face as he slumped forward or my own horror as he fell. By now, a large crowd was running toward me from every direction. There were no military weapons on these farmer-militiamen, but they carried knives, long, sharp-pointed sticks, and machetes wired to poles prepared for just such an occasion. Everyone was shouting in a cacophony of Vietnamese curses and threats. They stopped about fifteen feet from me and formed a ring, completely blocking my escape. They could see the young man in the water at my feet and were afraid to come any closer. I circled, aiming my gun towards each man as I turned. We were at a strange impasse—each eyeing the other—each afraid.

Perhaps a minute passed. During those long seconds, I realized this was going to be my final appearance on the earth. It was perhaps the first time I had seriously contemplated death. Then an old, gray-haired Vietnamese stepped out from the ring.

I bore down on him with the 38. He dropped his machete and put his arms down at his side. Then he raised them for silence. The crowd obeyed and an eerie silence followed. The next two minutes were critical for me. I couldn't speak Vietnamese; he couldn't speak English. But through gestures and signs, he promised me that if I would not shoot again, he, their leader, would guarantee my safety.

To this day I cannot believe that those few wild gestures could make that complex message clear. Looking back, I believe the hands of God were gesturing through the hands of my enemy to save my life, and I am grateful.

Realizing that to trust the old man was the best of some very bad options, I threw my five remaining shells as far as I could in one direction and the revolver in the other. If they were going to kill me, it wouldn't be with my survival weapon.

Then, the brief silence was broken by a unison scream of revenge, and the crowd was on me. They pounded me to my knees. I felt a shower of blows on my head and shoulders from their bamboo clubs. Each man and boy, feeling years of pent-up anger and hatred, took this moment of revenge. Each got his blow, and for a moment I feared that I had made the wrong decision. I had been deceived. Then—just before unconsciousness—the old man intervened. The blows and kicks and curses ceased, and I was dragged to my feet.

At that moment the village commissar arrived, wielding a vintage German luger. His was the first uniform I had seen that day, and he was obviously in charge. He took one arm, the old man took the other, and together they half-dragged, half-walked me toward the village. In the confusion a boy about twelve years old slipped out of the crowd, deftly lifted my watch right off my arm and ran off with it. Later in the crowd I saw him passing out the twenty-dollar bills I had been carrying in my flight jacket. He had no idea how much those green bills were worth.

The crowd was jubilant. They had captured a valuable prisoner. They were returning to their village in triumph. Suddenly, I felt afraid. Everyone was looking toward the village. Instinctively, I looked backward and saw, to my horror, a man, his face twisted in anger, running towards me. A huge scar ran down the right side of his face; his right eye was missing; he was running at me full-tilt, carrying a three-foot-long rusty harpoon. He had every intention of planting that lance deep into my back. I lunged in front of the commissar who, upon realizing my predicament, felled the man with one strong blow to the face with that old German luger. What made me feel the danger and turn? I believe it was God at work again.

By now we had crossed to the edge of the village. The whole town had gathered. For a moment they just stood and looked at this strange man from another world. They were peasants dressed uniformly in simple, black, pajama outfits. I stood before them in full-battle dress, armed with a flare gun, sheath knives, a two-way radio, life vest, compass, navigational watch, and miscellaneous survival paraphernalia. I must have looked like a man from the moon to them. For one long moment we stood in open-mouthed unbelief seeing each other close up for the first time. Then they laid me spread-eagle on the dirt path and commenced to undress me and relieve me of my treasures.

They didn't use any of the zippers on my flight clothing. They took knives and machetes and cut off everything, including my boots. In seconds I was completely naked. Someone tossed me short, ragged pants and a child's short-sleeved shirt with no buttons. I struggled into my new uniform and sat back exhausted on a low rock wall, wiped my arm across my face and was quite surprised when it came back covered with blood. I must have been a sight, almost naked, covered with mud, beaten to a pulp, my leg wounded and bleeding.

The commissar held the crowd back, unsure what to do with his unexpected prize. Then the crowd parted and a little Vietnamese man approached carrying a black medic bag. A woman followed with a basin of water. Together they washed my wounds, wrapped a bandage around my head, and gave me a shot in each arm. I recognized the syringe of morphine from my survival gear and supposed the other was a tetanus shot. This moment of compassion that probably saved my life seemed even then an act of God. These people had every reason to hate me. If it hadn't been for the commissar, I believe they would have killed me on the spot. This medic went about his work without a smile or friendly gesture as if compelled by a force of compassion that outweighed any hatred and desire for revenge.

When the medic finished his hasty repairs, the commissar dragged me through the crowd to a little shelter just off the central village square. I lay on my back on a hard, wooden pallet on the dirt floor. The room was dark, with no windows; a kerosene lamp burned nearby, lighting the room in flickering semi-darkness. All afternoon and into the night the commissar let the villagers enter the room in groups of three or four. No one showed particular hostility. They were mainly curious. No one did me any harm. Now and then a teen-ager would spit on me, say something in anger, and punch me with his finger, I suppose to tell his young friends he had touched the fallen American pilot. Few tried to speak. Most simply looked, then hurried on. I thought of funerals back in Tulsa and how mourners approached the casket, stared for a moment, and then walked on. This time the corpse stared back. Then the crowds stopped coming. I was alone for the first time since my capture. I had not thought about God much since dropping out of Sunday school in my late teens, but lying on the floor, I could not help but think of Him then.

I had come close to death so many times in that one day and each time I had felt the hand of God. Pictures flooded my mind: the plane exploding into a ball of flame moments after I had ejected—shots zinging by me, making holes in my parachute—the crowd of angry men beating and kicking me, intent upon my death—that unforgettable face twisted by anger and by war, running at me with the rusty lance—the medic—the commissar—the old man.

I was a prisoner of war. I had no idea what my fate would be, but the Lord had made Himself abundantly clear. He was there with me in the presence of my enemies, and I breathed my second prayer of thanks that day.

2

New Guy Village

My first day in captivity had left me exhausted but grateful to be alive. I had survived the day on grace and my adrenalin. Now, the adrenalin was wearing off, and the morphine was taking hold. My thoughts slowed to a halt, and I floated in a drugged stupor on the floor of that village shelter. A loud commotion in the village square jolted me back to my senses. It was the sound of a crowd of cheering peasants running along behind a large truck. The truck stopped outside.

The door burst open, and in marched eight or nine North Vietnamese regular soldiers in army uniforms. They hauled me to my feet. It was then I learned my badly sprained leg could not support my weight, so the soldiers dragged me between them through the crowd outside. There were no electric lights in the village, but makeshift torches lit the night. The people cheered the soldiers as they loaded me onto the back of a half-ton military truck. I lay spread-eagle on the slats, while one young soldier blindfolded me and lay a tarpaulin over my shivering body. Unfortunately, the tarpaulin wasn't meant for warmth but to guarantee that I could not see anything on the coming journey.

The truck pulled out of that village and sped toward Hanoi.

We drove the entire night on a very rough road, stopping every few hours for the soldiers to unveil me to another cluster of applauding peasants carrying torches and cheering the soldiers loudly. One particular stop was unforgettable. There were no crowds this time; in fact, we were parked on a pontoon bridge in the middle of a wide river. The soldiers took off my blindfold and pointed thirty feet above me to the Ham Rong bridge which they thought had been my target. It was still standing. I noticed that our truck's wheels were submerged beneath the water and that the pontoon bridge was totally hidden from the surface to camouflage it. My enemy was proud, and boisterous, and confident.

At about dawn the next morning, I could hear traffic and the sounds of a city. The truck stopped and my blindfold was removed; then, we drove into a large fortress in the heart of Hanoi, In the few seconds I had to survey my surroundings, it was perfectly clear that this was a prison that would permit no escape.

A series of huge concrete walls fifteen to twenty feet high surrounded the inner buildings. Broken glass was cemented into the surface, and hot, electric wires ran the length of the walls. There was a dry moat around the prison separating one tall wall from the other.

We drove through iron gates and stopped before an ominous structure of concrete brick and mortar approximately thirty-five feet long and twenty-five feet wide. Inside this tomblike building were eight individual cells, 6 x 6 feet. Each held two concrete bunks, one on each side, with barely enough room to walk between them. The bunks were about two feet wide and at the bottom of each, imbedded in cement, was a set of iron stocks. A prisoner would put his feet in place, and another iron bar was forced down across the top with an iron pin to lock them. There were seven cells with an eighth prepared as a kind of washing place. This was Heartbreak Hotel. It was one of many cell blocks of the huge Hoa Lo prison complex. Built by the French early in the century, American aircrews housed there had nicknamed the prison the "Hanoi Hilton." Needless to say, this was no hotel.

I saw no other prisoners as I was dragged into Cell 7. Only minutes passed before the guards moved me again from Heart-break Hotel into a completely different section of the prison. Later I learned my second stop was nicknamed New Guy Village, for almost every new prisoner was housed temporarily in its cells.

The retaining room I now found myself in had knobby plaster walls that gave the place a cavelike appearance. Nicknamed the "Knobby Room," it was small and the filthiest place I had seen to date. It was like the worst of slums in miniature. I sat down on a pile of debris in the center of this mess and took stock of my condition.

I had no clothes. I was freezing cold. I had eaten nothing for twenty-four exhausting hours. My body ached. My leg and wrist were sprained and swelling badly. I was covered with caked blood and filth. The officers' quarters on the *Bon Homme Richard,* a warm bath, a hot cup of coffee, that emergency first-aid kit I hadn't opened in ten years seemed a million miles away.

No sooner had I begun to collect my thoughts than I was interrupted by a burly Vietnamese officer who led me from the Knobby Room into an interrogation center nearby. I knew this moment was coming. I had been trained in survival school and was well versed in the Code of Conduct. I was to answer only four questions. The questions began almost politely.

"Your name?"

"Howard Rutledge," I answered, teeth chattering in the morning chill.

"Your rank and serial number?" he continued.

"Commander; 506435," I replied.

"Your date of birth?"

"13 November 1928."

The questions continued without pause. "Your squadron and ship?"

I refused to answer further, explaining the American fighting man's code and the International Conventions at Geneva, 1949.

His reply was calm and quiet. "You are not a prisoner of war," he said. "Your government has not declared war upon the Vietnamese people. You must answer my questions. You are protected by no international law." I continued to refuse to answer any of his questions.

Suddenly, the interrogator closed his notebook, leaned over toward me and said, "Commander Rutledge, you are a criminal, guilty of high crimes against the Vietnamese people. If you do not answer my questions, you will be severely punished."

With that I was led back into the Knobby Room and given thirty minutes to decide. The guard returned, and I was taken back into the interrogation room and asked the first four questions, which I answered again. The fifth I refused to answer. I was threatened again and returned to the Knobby Room. This little charade happened every thirty minutes for the entire day. The verbal lashings increased each time I refused to cooperate. But every time I returned to the Knobby Room, I felt I had beaten them again.

Meanwhile my body ached with growing ferocity. I had received no clothing, and I was beginning to "cold soak." My body temperature was dropping to the temperature of the North Vietnamese winter evening; my swollen wrist and leg were throbbing, but I was going to win. Survival school had taught me well. Again I was called to the interrogation room.

This time when I refused to answer the threat of punishment sounded like a promise. "Now, Commander Rutledge," the interrogator said, "you will be severely punished."

I was taken back to the Knobby Room. The officer who spoke English was joined by a guard we named Pigeye and three men in civilian clothes. Pigeye probably tortured more Americans than any other North Vietnamese. The others looked like criminals off the street. A guard with a burp gun closed the door on the six of us and stood watching through the bars.

The officer told me to sit on the floor and extend my legs straight out. My left leg was so badly swollen that I could not straighten it, so one of the interrogator's accomplices planted his heavy boot on my knee and forced the swollen leg onto the cement floor. I felt a flash of pain and simultaneously felt my leg pop. That guard probably did me a real favor by forcing into place my badly dislocated leg. It may seem strange to thank God for this sadistic act, but I don't know what would have happened to my leg if that guard hadn't acted.

Then they forced my legs into spurlike shackles and used a pipe and strong rope to lock both ankles firmly into place. Next they forced my arms into a long-sleeved shirt and began to tie them behind me from above my elbows to my wrists. One guard put his foot on my back, forcing the laces tight enough to cut off all circulation and pulling my shoulder blades almost apart. I could see the rope cut through my wrists all the way to the bone, but they did not bleed, because the bindings acted like a tourniquet, cutting off circulation entirely into my arms and hands.

I began to have severe pains in my arms; by forcing myself on my side, I could see my arms and hands had turned a deep shade of blue. It slowly dawned on me that they were going to leave me in this miserable position until I answered their questions. For a while I thought that I would die. I never prayed for death, but I did pray for unconsciousness. For at least three hours I lay in this position, my prayer unanswered.

Then the guards returned, unlaced my arms and legs, and left again. I had a terrible fear that my arms would never function normally, but an hour or so later feeling began to return, and except for deep cuts and bruises they soon moved quite normally. My first contact with torture as a weapon of war had left me a

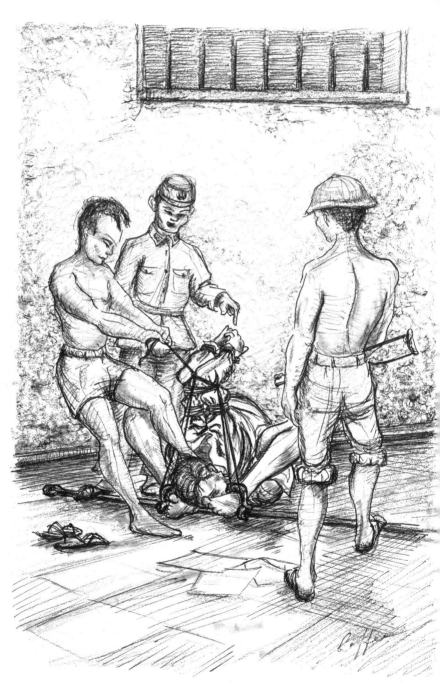

One guard put his foot on my back, forcing the laces tight enough to cut off all circulation and pulling my shoulder blades almost apart.

bit unnerved, and when they brought me once again to the interrogation room, it took all the strength I could muster to refuse to answer their questions once again.

All they wanted was for me to answer question number five— my squadron, airwing, and ship. If I didn't answer, I would be hogtied again and probably lose the use of my arms and hands, if not my life.

"Commander Rutledge, you have committed high crimes against our people. You will be severely punished if you do not answer our questions."

My explanation was interrupted; I was returned to the Knobby Room, placed in shackles, tightly bound, and left again to ponder my resistance. This time the guards slapped me several times before they left. And each time during the night, as I refused to answer, their blows increased. Around dawn the interrogator was relieved by a high-ranking officer. Later I learned the prisoners called him Colonel Nam.

I had been through an entire night of punishment, and the more I had refused, the more angry and impatient everyone had become. Now, everyone was tense and angry. When Colonel Nam repeated the questions and then the threats, I exploded in anger.

"Why don't you go ahead and kill me, because I will *not* answer your questions!" Colonel Nam did not reply. He just watched as the guards dragged me away. This time they would have their answers.

I was shackled; the laces were pulled unbearably tight. I had not eaten for two days, and my requests for medical care for my wrist and legs and head were ignored. I had not even been permitted to have a normal kidney or bowel movement in the entire time. I still had no clothes and was truly cold.

This time they laced the rope from my ankles up around my neck through my handcuffed wrists. This forced me into a pretzel-like position; if I bent forward or leaned backward, the rope would choke me. I had to sit in a perfectly upright position, with arms laced tightly behind my back. One guard repeatedly struck my head and shoulders with a bamboo pole; another jumped up and down on the rope binding my legs, cutting deep into my ankles. I prayed for unconsciousness. I asked God to give me strength. I thought about my wife Phyllis and my family, and knew I would never see them again. I knew my ability to endure any more physical or mental pain was rapidly ending. I determined that before I cracked completely, I would volunteer to answer their questions, hoping that while I still had some control, I could lie and deceive them and so survive.

"Stop." My voice was no more than a whisper. "I will answer."

Immediately, they undid my bindings and unshackled me. As I lay there on the floor, the interrogator entered and politely asked me question number five.

"What is your service?" he said.

"The United States Navy," I replied.

Then he was gone. They had their fifth answer. It was all they wanted.

Guards brought a blanket and a suit of long prison clothes. At last I was allowed to relieve myself. I could not eat. I received no medical attention, not even Mercurochrome, but I lay back on that concrete slab and slept.

3

Heartbreak Hotel

On the morning of December 1, 1965, two guards roused me from a fitful sleep and marched me out of New Guy Village across the prison into Cell 2, Heartbreak Hotel. When the door slammed and the key turned in that rusty, iron lock, a feeling of utter loneliness swept over me. I lay down on that cold cement slab in my 6 x 6 prison. The smell of human excrement burned my nostrils. A rat, large as a small cat, scampered across the slab beside me. The walls and floors and ceilings were caked with filth. Bars covered a tiny window high above the door. I was cold and hungry; my body ached from the swollen joints and sprained muscles.

I felt guilty for having answered more. Worst of all, I felt totally alone. I seldom cry, but that day tears of self-pity and of fear welled up in my eyes, and I fought them back. This was my first taste of solitary confinement. The war against my nerves had begun.

Then I heard a voice.

"New guy that just moved in, what's your name? What ship are you from?"

I literally sprang to that window and pressed my face against the cold iron bars. Down the narrow passageway staring back at me were other Americans. Commander James Stockdale, air-wing commander downed in September had spoken. I was not alone!

At great personal risk he briefed me quickly and clearly about the other men in Heartbreak. In a cell across the way was Commander Harry Jenkins, a squadron commander in Airwing 16. To the left was Air Force Captain George McNight, downed only weeks before. In Cell 4 was Lt. Comdr. Duffy Hutton from a photo-recon squadron, and across from him Marine Captain Harley Chapman off the attack carrier USS *Oriskany*, and Air Force Lt. Jerry Singleton, a helicopter pilot downed in November.

In quiet, rapid phrases, Commander Stockdale told me that to clear the area of guards, the person wanting to communicate would whistle "Mary Had a Little Lamb." Everyone would immediately get down on his hands and knees and look through a small crack under his door to insure that his own immediate space was clear of guards. If you saw a Vietnamese in the corridor, you'd cough, the danger signal not to communicate.

Then I spoke. The words poured out of me. I was a traitor. I had answered more questions than name, rank, serial number, and date of birth.

Commander Stockdale heard my brief confession. When I had finished he simply said, "Don't feel like the Lone Ranger." Someone coughed; then all was silent.

The silence lasted throughout the entire day and night that followed. Soon I learned that communication was risky business. We could get off only snatches of conversation in an entire day. The rest of the time we sat alone in our cells. It's hard to describe what solitary confinement can do to unnerve and defeat a man. You quickly tire of standing up or sitting down, sleeping or being awake. There are no books, no paper or pencils, no magazines or newspapers. The only colors you see are drab gray and dirty brown. Months or years may go by when you don't see the sunrise or the moon, green grass or flowers. You are locked in, alone

I literally sprang to that window and pressed my face against
the cold iron bars.

and silent in your filthy little cell breathing stale, rotten air and trying to keep your sanity.

I remembered Edgar Allan Poe's vision of hell in "The Pit and the Pendulum." Poe's hero saw the walls slowly moving toward him, threatening to crush him to death. In Heartbreak Hotel I realized Poe's walls may not have moved at all. It is something in one's head that moves to crush him. I had the best of survival training in the navy, and it got me through that first long day of interrogation. But after that I was alone, and no survival training can prepare a man for years of solitary confinement. What sustains a man in prison is something that he has going for him inside his heart and head—something that happened, or did not happen—back in childhood in the home and church and school. Nobody can teach you to survive the brutality of being alone. At first you panic. You want to cry out. You fight back waves of fear. You want to die, to confess, to do anything to get out of that ever-shrinking world. Then, gradually a plan of defense takes shape. Being alone is another kind of war, but slowly I learned that it, too, can be won. Like a blind man who is forced to develop other senses to replace his useless eyes, a man in solitary confinement must quit regretting what he cannot do and build a new life around what he can do.

Since I couldn't move more than a few feet in any direction, I lay on my bunk and moved my eyes, searching out interesting cracks or scratches in the plaster. Who had made them? What could they mean? Immediately I learned that though no human being shared my tiny space, I was not really alone. The walls were crawling with interesting vermin. Ants fascinated me, and even the rats made entertaining though ugly roommates. These North Vietnamese rats were unlike any I had ever seen; they were over a foot long and looked like opossums. One old rat was so big I fantasized his stepping out into the corridor and calling, "Here, Kitty, Kitty!" Because I couldn't force myself to eat the bowl of cold seaweed soup with sowbelly fat on the top and could only nibble at the stale French loaf during those first lonely days, my cell was preferred territory to these large, ugly rodents.

More friendly and more agile than the rats were the geckos, six-to-nine-inch-long multicolored lizards with suction cups on their legs. These prehistoric little monsters were wonderful entertainment. They could dart across a wall and snatch an unsuspecting fly or mosquito in mid-flight. I played a game with geckos; lying on my slab, I tried to herd the flies in their direction, celebrating every gecko conquest and keeping score, competing one gecko's accuracy against another.

I developed all kinds of mental games that kept me entertained and edified by the hours. In those thirty-four days in Heartbreak, I also disciplined myself to reconstruct my life, year by year, month by month, day by day. I worked hard to reconstruct and evaluate each event. My memory had rusted over, and I set about scraping the rust away.

In prison I discovered how important regular times of reflection can be. Living in America, one becomes preoccupied with family and career. When I was free, I seldom thought seriously about what I was doing or why I was doing it. When days are filled by travel, conversation, books, papers, movies, television, meals, radio, billboards, and the like, the mind is constantly looking outward and dealing with the world outside and around. But when suddenly all that is taken away, it is forced to deal with the world inside.

At first, this process of remembering was torture; all I could think about was food. I thought of Wednesday steak night in the officers' mess on the *Bon Homme Richard:* a six-inch baked potato swimming in butter, sour cream, and chives; hot apple pie with cheese and hot coffee, all I could drink. I thought of Mom's chocolate pie or my wife's cooking—anything and everything she put on the table. Then I would see the bowl of rotting pumpkin or seaweed soup and the small loaf of stale French bread in my cell. The thought of swallowing that cold, greasy, repugnant stuff was nauseating. Day by day I refused to eat until my own body fat had been depleted, and my weight began to drop. Soon it became clear that if I didn't eat, I would starve. If I didn't get the necessary protein, I could not survive. Already I was weak and getting weaker.

One day I decided to eat it all. I never really felt full the entire seven years in Vietnam; but every bite of seaweed soup, every small piece of sowbelly fat, every bowl of sewer greens kept me a little closer to health and survival. When one is dying from starvation, a bowl of sewer greens is a gift from God. Before every meal during my captivity, I offered a prayer of thanks. In the past, when others prayed my mind wandered over the day's events or simply waited impatiently for the prayer to end. But in prison, grace was not a routine endured out of habit, guilt, or pressure. To thank God for life seemed the natural thing to do.

During those long periods of enforced reflection, it became so much easier to separate the important from the trivial, the worthwhile from the waste. For example, in the past, I usually worked or played hard on Sundays and had no time for church. For years Phyllis encouraged me to join the family at church. She never nagged or scolded—she just kept hoping. But I was too busy, too preoccupied, to spend one or two short hours a week thinking about the really important things.

Now the sights and sounds and smells of death were all around me. My hunger for spiritual food soon outdid my hunger for a steak. Now I wanted to know about that part of me that will never die. Now I wanted to talk about God and Christ and the church. But in Heartbreak solitary confinement there was no pastor, no Sunday-school teacher, no Bible, no hymnbook, no community of believers to guide and sustain me. I had completely neglected the spiritual dimension of my life. It took prison to show me how empty life is without God, and so I had to go back in my memory to those Sunday-school days in the Nogales Avenue Baptist Church, Tulsa, Oklahoma. If I couldn't have a Bible and hymnbook, I would try to rebuild them in my mind.

I tried desperately to recall snatches of Scripture, sermons, the gospel choruses from childhood, and the hymns we sang in church. The first three dozen songs were relatively easy. Every day I'd try to recall another verse or a new song. One night there was a huge thunderstorm—it was the season of the monsoon rains—and a bolt of lightning knocked out the lights and plunged the entire prison into darkness. I had been going over hymn tunes in my mind and stopped to lie down and sleep when the rains began to fall. The darkened prison echoed with wave after wave of water. Suddenly, I was humming my thirty-seventh song, one I had entirely forgotten since childhood.

> Showers of blessings,
> Showers of blessing we need!
> Mercy drops round us are falling,
> But for the showers we plead.

I no sooner had recalled those words than another song popped into my mind, the theme song of a radio program my mother listened to when I was just a kid.

> Heavenly sunshine, heavenly sunshine
> Flooding my soul with glory divine.
> Heavenly sunshine, heavenly sunshine.
> Hallelujah! Jesus is mine!

Most of my fellow prisoners were struggling like me to rediscover faith, to reconstruct workable value systems. Harry Jenkins lived in a cell nearby during much of my captivity. Often we would use those priceless seconds of communication in a day to help one another recall Scripture verses and stories.

One day I heard him whistle. When the cell block was clear, I waited for his communication, thinking it to be some important news. "I got a new one," he said. "I don't know where it comes from or why I remember it, but it's a story about Ruth and Naomi." He then went on to tell that ancient story of Ruth following Naomi into a hostile new land and finding God's presence and protection there. Harry's urgent news was two thousand years old. It may not seem important to prison life, but we lived off that story for days, rebuilding it, thinking about what it meant, and applying God's ancient words to our predicament.

Everyone knew the Lord's Prayer and the Twenty-Third Psalm, but the camp favorite verse that everyone recalled first and quoted most often is found in the Book of John, third chapter, sixteenth verse.

> For God so loved the world, that he gave his only begotten Son, that whosoever believeth in him should not perish, but have everlasting life.

With Harry's help I even reconstructed the seventeenth and eighteenth verses.

> For God sent not his Son into the world to condemn the world; but that the world through him might be saved. He that believeth on him is not condemned: but he that believeth not is condemned already, because he hath not believed in the name of the only begotten Son of God.

How I struggled to recall those Scriptures and hymns! I had spent my first eighteen years in a Southern Baptist Sunday school, and I was amazed at how much I could recall; regrettably, I had not seen then the importance of memorizing verses from the Bible or learning gospel songs. Now, when I needed them, it was too late. I never dreamed that I would spend almost seven years (five of them in solitary confinement) in a prison in North Vietnam or that thinking about one memorized verse could have made a whole day bearable. One portion of a verse I did remember was, "Thy word have I hid in my heart." How often I wished I had really worked to hide God's Word in my heart. I put my mind to work. Every day I planned to accomplish certain tasks. I woke early, did my physical exercises, cleaned up as best I could, then began a period of devotional prayer and meditation. I would pray, hum hymns silently, quote Scripture, and think about what the verses meant to me.

Remember, we weren't playing games. The enemy knew that the best way to break a man's resistance was to crush his spirit in a lonely cell. In other wars, some of our POWs after solitary confinement lay down in a fetal position and died. All this talk of Scripture and hymns may seem boring to some, but it was the way we conquered our enemy and overcame the power of death around us.

It looked as though I would spend my first Christmas in captivity in Heartbreak Hotel; but about 8 P.M. Christmas Eve, 1965, guards entered my cell, blindfolded me, roped me into a jeep with Lt. Commander Duffy Hutton, and drove us across Hanoi to another prison. POWs called it the Zoo, and it would be my home for two torturously long years.

4

The Zoo

To the southwest of downtown Hanoi, there is an old French art colony complete with race track, swimming pool, theater, and assorted living quarters, and service buildings. It must have been quite a showplace at the height of French colonialism. However, by that Christmas Eve, 1965, when I was taken there, some changes had been made.

American prisoners had named this art-colony-turned-prison, the Zoo. Around the place there was a foreboding wall, with guard towers and massive gates. The outbuildings had been stripped of furnishings, the windows had been bricked over, bars covered any opening that remained, individual cells had been constructed in every building, the pool was being used to grow fish for camp officials, the place was overgrown with weeds, and piles of filth were crawling with vermin and rodents. Each building had a name that best indicated the change: the Stable, the Outhouse, and the Pigsty.

Our guards took off our blindfolds and marched me to the Pigsty where I first met the English-speaking interrogator POWs called the Dog. He was large for a Vietnamese and wore a Chinese-type cap with a red star; a cardboard collar-insignia on his olive-drab uniform indicated his rank. I immediately recognized the hated Pigeye standing at his side. It would not be long before I experienced his torture skills again.

The Dog asked me my name and rank. Hoping there might be other Americans present, I shouted out my reply, "Commander Howard Rutledge!" He scribbled on a yellow pad and walked away. Seconds passed.

Then, in the darkness I heard a voice. "Commander Rutledge, come towards the front window." Commander Bill Franke had heard me call out my name. Quickly and quietly he explained where I was. Because it was dark, he couldn't clear the area of guards but promised to communicate the next day.

Cell 4, Pigsty, was approximately 15 x 15 feet. It seemed huge after one month in the closet at Heartbreak. But there was no bed or furnishings, just a cold cement floor. The windows had not yet been bricked in on Cell 4, and the winter cold made my prison feel like an icehouse. Still, I lay back on that cement floor with some hope. After all, I was "on the line"—communicating within thirty seconds of my arrival.

I'll not forget that first Christmas Eve in captivity. It was terribly cold, and though I knew of at least one other American nearby, I was still alone. My body still ached, and my wounds were only beginning to heal. As I lay there in my ice-cold misery, somewhere in my cell a Christmas carol began to play. It was an incredible surprise; I sat up and searched the cell. For a moment I thought my mind was playing treacherous tricks— "Silent Night, Holy Night." The fidelity was awful, but it was the first song I had heard since bailing out more than a month ago. Scratches and all, that carol was beautiful beyond describing.

Then the carol ended, and the voice of Hanoi Hanna came on with a barrage of propaganda. Later I learned that in the walls every cell had a speaker that broadcast bizarre programming for the prisoners. Many of the programs were recorded in the United States, and were designed to agitate homesick Americans. "Radio Stateside" may have been a tool to break us down, but the snatches of American music, especially that carol on Christmas Eve, backfired and really boosted my spirits.

I hadn't thought about Christmas carols for my growing list of hymns and gospel songs, but on that strange Christmas Eve, with Hanoi Hanna ranting in the background, I recalled at least eight or ten carols, verse by verse. It was like discovering hidden treasure, and I reveled in it.

On Christmas morning we were awakened early by the camp gong. I hadn't shaved in thirty-two days, and my hair was dirty and extra-long. I was taken to the bathing area and given a haircut and shave. It was primitive but rejuvenating. Americans were not allowed to mix, so the one-by-one trip to the latrine took all of Christmas morning.

Around noon in North Vietnam, the turnkeys (jailers) take a nap. The minimal crew of guards was fairly easy to clear, and in that short hour we could communicate with others without great fear of being caught and punished.

Because I was the new guy at the Zoo, immediately upon clearing the area, everyone wanted to know the latest news from the outside world.

Commander Franke, imprisoned already for five to six months, peered through the crack above his door and whispered the question everyone wanted answered.

"When do you think the war will end?"

Later I learned that across the way listening was Everett Alvarez, the first American POW, downed eighteen months before. How could I tell them it might go on for years? I tried to give them a straightforward message that wouldn't shatter spirits and destroy morale.

"Hang on. We might be here next Christmas."

I could hear the groan pass from cell to cell. Immediately I felt guilty for bringing such bad news, especially at Christmas.

Even I never dreamed it would be seven more long years before release.

The next question Bill Franke asked me was, "Do you know the code?"

The first regulation in all the prisons of North Vietnam was DO NOT COMMUNICATE WITH YOUR FELLOW AMERICANS. The enemy knew that if he could isolate a man—make him feel abandoned—cut off—forgotten—he could more easily destroy his resistance and break down his morale. To win this war against our nerves, we had to devise all kinds of ingenious systems to keep the lines open among our fellow prisoners. We learned to think like criminals, to devise ways to lie, cheat, and deceive.

The tap code Commander Franke asked me about was a series of taps and pauses, representing each letter in the alphabet. A man would get down on his hands and knees, wrap himself in a blanket to cut down noise a guard might hear, and tap out messages to the man in an adjoining cell. This man would receive the message, then pass it on to the man next door. Sometimes a message could sweep around the cell block faster than a guard could walk.

"Yes, Bill, I know the code." I had overheard the code being whispered to another prisoner during my short stay at Heartbreak and had memorized it, never realizing I would spend the next seven years using this simple code to tap out messages almost every day.

Communicating was our major weapon against the enemy. Each cell block had a key man who initiated most communication efforts. He usually was located in a place which allowed him the best view of the area. When he gave the signal to clear, each of us would scramble for a position to see if any guards were about. If there were two men in a cell, one would climb on the other's shoulders and look through the high, transom-like windows above the solid wooden doors. Though most of us were kept in solitary confinement, it was advantageous for many

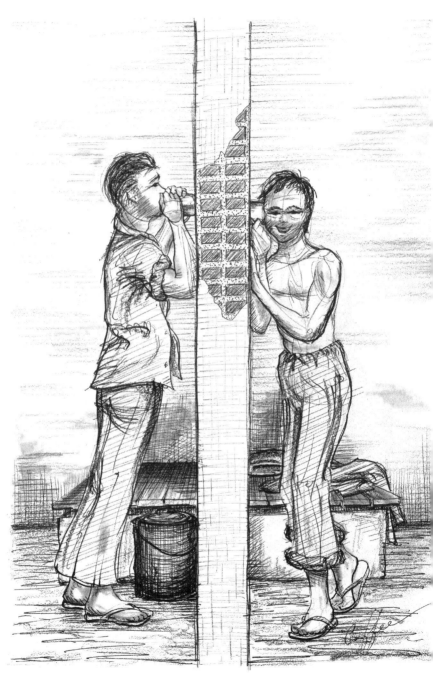

Our little tin drinking cups, issued by the enemy, served as effective transducers to get voice or tapped messages through solid walls.

reasons to be with another prisoner. You could send messages on the wall, while the other maintained security. Many prisoners in solitary risked punishment daily to send messages and keep the line clear. Often in the midst of communicating, a lone prisoner would be surprised by a guard and severely punished.

Our little tin drinking cups, issued by the enemy, served as effective transducers to get voice or tap messages through solid, cement walls. Every time a new man would enter a prison, his name and rank would be passed quickly to the entire camp and memorized. That way we protected each other. If we knew each other's names, the enemy could not lie or claim they never knew us. I can still reel off more than four hundred names and serial numbers memorized in prison.

That Christmas Day was memorable for more than my first bath and shave. We were fed a turkey dinner. There were many pictures taken by the enemy that day to show how well we were being treated. But perhaps a year went by between those few real meals that we had.

That first New Year's Day of captivity I made at least three resolutions that I repeated each year:

1. I would try never to be cold again.
2. I would try never to be hungry again.
3. I would never be without the Bible again. (This I would put in my mind and my heart.)

Early in January the Dog asked me for a written autobiographical sketch. Surprisingly, when I refused, he let me go. I was moved from the Pigsty down to a small, solitary cell with no windows where I remained alone until August 1966. Living in a cement box with cement floors, cement walls, and bricked-in windows is like living in a cold-storage vault in the winter and a hotbox in the summer.

Alone in the cell, I continued my devotional periods searching my mind for Scriptures, going over the more than fifty hymns I had recalled. My wrist and leg were almost back to normal. In spite of almost no medical care, my cuts and bruises from the first interrogation had healed. I knew my turn for interrogation would come again. I waited and wondered when.

Early in August the guards came for me. They took me to the "Auditorium," an old theater dressing room, and again the Dog demanded that I write a confession and a biographical sketch. When I refused, they shackled me to the spot and left. A tiny bulb was the only source of light in this spooky torture room. As my eyes became accustomed to the dimness, I could see spiders as big as my fist hanging all around me. They may have been friendly spiders, but they created quite a terrifying effect in the semidarkness. Ants crawled all over me, and nine million mosquitoes were trapped inside. Gecko lizards scurried through the filth, and large rats looked me over hungrily. It is a helpless sensation to be shackled, hands and feet, in such a place. I had no way to kill the mosquitoes or frighten off the rats. I just sat and watched and trembled.

I sat for four days and nights hardly moving. I remember the third day, August 7, because for two days and nights it had been stifling hot. The third day it rained and those showers of blessings cooled off the cell, and made it almost bearable. Also, August 7 was the day I married Phyllis eighteen years before. Was she well? Did she know I was alive? I missed her so. I breathed a prayer that God would get us through and, if He willed, let me hold her in my arms again.

Each day the Dog or Spot, his assistant, came in to demand a confession, anything in writing the enemy could use against us. I continued to refuse, and on August 8, 1966, the Dog visited me again and insisted once more upon my writing a confession or this time to suffer the punishment of death.

I took the pen, and wrote my choice on the paper, and handed it back to him. DEATH!

They slapped me around and cursed and threatened and demanded something useful in writing.

So I took the pen and wrote again. "I support my country, its government, and its people. I always will." Then I signed it.

August 8, 1966, Pigeye and his friends shackled me, hands and feet, in another torture room, dubbed by those who suffered there, the Outhouse. The Outhouse was located on the south wall of the camp just behind Pigsty. It was a squat, flat-roofed, concrete, bunkerlike room with no windows. The filth in that small room was far beyond anything I had seen to date. In fact, the ants were so plentiful and so large that I am sure by now they've eaten up the entire cement building.

Because it was out in the sun, the temperature inside—and I believe I'm estimating conservatively—was 100 or 110 degrees at midnight.

As I sat there in a pile of human excrement crawling with countless moving things, I thought back upon my "bravery." It was not bravery to ask for death when the enemy needed us alive, but I knew the cost I would pay for my resistance. Again it took all the courage I could muster. Now I sat staring into the darkness, gagging on the odor, my skin crawling with pests that bit and pinched in the dark. My courage waned. Maybe they wouldn't kill me. Maybe they would just abuse me until I died.

I remained in the Outhouse, my hands cuffed behind my back, my legs in irons. They gave me only a small bowl of rice each day and two cups of filthy water. It was unbearably hot, and by the end of the first week I was very sick with dysentery and couldn't eat. For almost three weeks I sat getting weaker each day from the constant diarrhea and the lack of food and water. There was a bucket in the room in which to perform the bodily functions, but it is difficult when you're handcuffed with your arms behind your back and your legs in irons, and you're too weak to move. So I and the prisoners before me just relieved

ourselves in our clothing and on the floor. No one ever cleaned
the Outhouse. To keep us lying in that filth was part of the plan.

By the third week I had developed a heat rash that itched and
bled, and left me feeling close to despair. Our camp policy was
to hold on until just short of losing touch with reality and then
volunteer to confess in writing. While we still had some senses
left, we could usually write a confession anyone but our enemy
could tell was false. I decided that if each of us could take thirty
days in that torture room in one year, only twelve would suffer,
and some men might even be spared.

Each night was getting harder and harder to endure. I would
work my mind furiously in the daytime, hoping to be tired
enough at night to sleep in spite of heat rash, dysentery, hunger,
and pain. All day I planned to get through just one more night
and then confess, but in the morning I would feel new strength
to bear one more day and night.

On August 31, after twenty-eight days of torture, I could
remember I had children but not how many. I said Phyllis's
name over and over again so I would not forget. I prayed for
strength. It was on that twenty-eighth night I made God a promise. If I survived this ordeal, the first Sunday back in freedom I
would take Phyllis and my family to their church and at the
close of the service confess my faith in Christ and join the church.
This wasn't a deal with God to get me through that last miserable
night. It was a promise made after months of thought. It took
prison and hours of painful reflection to realize how much I
needed God and the community of believers. After I made God
that promise, again I prayed for strength to make it through the
night.

When the morning dawned through the crack in the bottom of
that solid prison door, I thanked God for His mercy and called
the guard.

Immediately upon hearing my willingness to write, the guards released me. I was taken to a bath and cleaned, then taken to the Fox, the commander of the Zoo, to sign my "confession."

"I am a Yankee imperialist aggressor," I wrote, parroting their text, knowing how little those words sounded like anything an American would write. I knew they had not released my name yet after nine months and that confession could be used against me to humiliate me in the camp and as propaganda around the world. I hoped my friends and family would understand.

5

Las Vegas

In January 1967 I left the Zoo with nineteen other men and traveled back across Hanoi to the Hanoi Hilton. The enemy had opened a new section, promptly dubbed *Las Vegas* by the prisoners, in the immense Hoa Lo prison complex. Six cell blocks ringed a courtyard area. On the north wall was the Thunderbird. On the Northeast corner was the Mint. Then came the Desert Inn and the Stardust along the east wall. The Riviera, on the south wall, and the Golden Nugget on the west completed the square.

In the courtyard were ten small bathing areas appropriately named the Sands. You can imagine what kind of baths they were. In fact, by May there was no water at all to fill the basins, so the enemy dug three wells in the Las Vegas courtyard. Because there was no sewer system, everything was dumped in holes beside the wells; therefore, the water we dipped to wash our clothes and to bathe was ultimately sewage, filthy with fungus and crawling with worms.

Inside each cell block was an assortment of cells ranging from 4-man units in a 9 x 9 foot space, to 2-men units in a 4 x 8 foot space, and in the Mint the smallest cells I had ever seen—total space 3 feet wide and just over 6 feet long. A hardwood bed on one wall left less than a 1 x 6 foot space to walk and exercise in.

At the foot of every bed in Las Vegas was a set of stocks to shackle an offending prisoner to his slab.

Apparently the enemy knew how effective our communication systems had become and had built Las Vegas to cut down our wall-tap system. They left a two-foot dead space between the cells so that prisoners could no longer share a common wall. We just continued tapping on the floor or common perimeter wall, and all their extra work didn't ever slow us down. We continued to communicate, to organize, and resist.

By now communication among the prisoners had become immensely effective. The enemy needed prisoner cooperation to make its propaganda tapes and to meet its press and protest delegations. The easiest victim was the new guy freshly captured who walked innocently into the enemy's trap. However, no sooner had the new guy entered the Hanoi Hilton than the prisoner-communication network got to him, briefed him on in-camp resistance policy, and turned him almost overnight into a seasoned resister.

During those long years of captivity, we learned to communicate with anything and everything. Under ideal circumstances—which seldom came—we could grab off a few minutes of face-to-face communications. As I explained earlier, we used tin cups as transducers to tap or talk coded messages through solid walls. For short distances we tapped with fingers; for longer distances we tapped with the ball of fist or elbows against the floor. Other legitimate noises were never wasted—a cough, a sniff, spitting, and/or clearing the throat were converted into simple communication efforts. One specially effective ruse was to sweep through a compound, using the broom movement to signal messages to the entire area. Or, if a man walked by another's cell, he could drag his little Ho-Chi-Minh sandals in code. When he cleaned out his "honey bucket," he swept and cleaned it with a bamboo broom. Often with the guards looking on, men pounded out messages on those pails with the enemy none the wiser.

We were shackled in our leg irons, handcuffed behind our backs in this position day and night.

We began to think like criminals. I have spent as much as ten hours a day staring at a two-inch drain hole trying to track and clear a guard so that I could grab five minutes of conversation on the wall. Tracking a guard revealed his habits, identified his routines. In two-man cells one prisoner sat on another's shoulder watching the guard, memorizing every regular move he made. When we had visual sightings of each other, we communicated with semaphore code or hand flash movements like the deaf use. If someone could see under the door opposite (through the crack), he could tap out messages with his toe to the prisoner across the corridor.

We even wrote coded messages to each other, using any scrap paper, including toilet paper, and writing with ink made of cigarette ashes or blood and water. We would take a piece of wire from a screen or a stick from the floor, tear off the bottom of old lead toothpaste rolls, and make a pencil. Charcoal and lye soap mixed together in the right proportions make an excellent crayon.

The enemy realized our communications system was beating them. We were isolated into small cells, yet the whole camp was organized and informed. I often fantasized about how I would enjoy taking a high North Vietnamese visitor through all the cell blocks, pointing out the name, rank, serial number, place of birth, date of capture, and even the favorite Scripture or food of every man in every cell block, even those areas I had never visited because through covert communications we could know almost that much.

However, our successes led eventually to painful reprisal. The enemy began a vicious crackdown, punishing men caught in the act of communicating with swift and unforgettable vengeance. There were small portholes in the cell doors; a guard could flip that door and catch a man without warning. Little child-size handcuffs would force the elbows together painfully, and we would be left in them for weeks at a time; or we were shackled in leg irons, handcuffed behind our backs, and left on our beds in this position day and night.

Later on, this cruelty was compounded by blindfolding a prisoner. If he cried out, he would be gagged with a rag. Also there were the little milking stools the prisoners sat on during interrogation. An offender would be forced to sit on the stool as long as he could, seven, maybe ten days. Of course, without sleep or rest, hallucinations start. If the offender moved, the guard would beat him. It was very severe punishment.

April 24, 1967, after only four months in Las Vegas, I was called to interrogation by an English-speaking officer we had dubbed the Rat. He surprised me with the news that after 540 days of solitary confinement I would have a roommate. That day I moved into Cell 6 of the Desert Inn, with Air Force Captain George McKnight, whom I had covertly talked with back in Heartbreak an eternity ago. Both of us were incorrigible. He had been at another camp near Hanoi, nicknamed the Briarpatch, and had suffered treatment similar to my own. Like my twenty-eight days in the Outhouse and the Auditorium, George had spent thirty-four days, hands cuffed behind his back, in a hole in the ground before he finally gave up and wrote his "confession."

For eighteen months I had experienced only snatches of covert conversation with anyone. He, too, had suffered under silence. The result was hilarious. We talked nonstop for three days and nights. In seventy-two hours of conversation, you can learn a lot about a man. One of the first things I asked him was, "George, do you know any Scripture?"

There was a long pause, and for a moment I thought I had landed a roommate totally uninterested in such things. Then slowly he replied, "No, I don't! I'm sorry." So during those next days together he listened to mine.

George is a bachelor. Apparently he was quite a swinger and called himself Peck's Bad Boy. But in prison he, too, had thought a lot about Christ and his church. He was a Catholic and had tied knots in a string to create a makeshift rosary. Every morning he would pray using the rosary, pacing in the little walk space we had. I would sit on the bed for my devotional.

Perhaps before I was shot down I had some prejudices against Catholics based on childhood misconceptions. I remembered talk of purgatory and limbo and the pope. But locked together in a tiny cell in a North Vietnamese prison, it didn't take the two of us long to get past such things that separated us to the common faith we felt in Christ.

Don't misunderstand. We weren't two fully-developed saints sitting dispassionately through the day discussing theology. There probably wasn't a thimbleful of serious theology between us. We just knew that without our faith in God, without our common belief that He was with us, we could not have made it through.

Prison life was rough. We were treated like animals, so, I am afraid, we developed some rather crude behavior in the process. One example was our constant use of four-letter words. Even covert communications were sometimes sprinkled with rough language. George and I both were quick-tempered and took pleasure in throwing out a curse to a guard. Because he couldn't understand English, we could smile and tell him in no uncertain terms how we felt about his brutality, and he had no idea how thoroughly he had been insulted. Swearing was one of the few pleasures we had. Nevertheless, we both knew that profanity was a crutch and a bad habit that needed breaking.

One day George and I made a pact. We would start on Sunday and go seven days; we would each keep track of the other's swear words, numbering them, and the person with the fewest slips would receive a precious banana at the end of the week. We may have had to steal the banana from a careless guard, but we weren't working on a cure for stealing that week!

After I had spent a year and a half alone, George McKnight, a Catholic brother-in-Christ, brought me new strength to face the years of prison that lay ahead. If I can help it, I will never try again to "go it alone." Those wild, hilarious, stimulating, prayerful nights of sharing we spent together in Las Vegas made me realize how much we need each other. The experience renewed my resolution made in the Outhouse, to join my family's church as one of my first acts upon reaching freedom and to take again my responsible place in Christ's body on earth.

On May 19 I was called before the senior interrogator at Las Vegas and asked to say something nice about prison treatment. I told him simply and clearly that the year and a half that Captain McKnight and I had spent in solitary confinement was the severest form of mental cruelty. Needless to say, he didn't take kindly to my remarks.

I'll not forget that night. Tensions were high. The heat had been miserable and our communications system was ruining the enemy's plans to use us in its propaganda war. The lights blinked on and off. Apparently the interrogator was a chain smoker, and cigarette rations were down, so he was trying in the semidarkness to roll his own. Suddenly our bombers struck Hanoi with unusual fury. The sirens sounded wildly, and the bombs began to fall around us, splitting the silence and rocking nearby targets. He exploded into a rage. I knew my days of living with the luxury of a roommate had ended. Two days later the guards entered my cell and took me to one of those 3 x 6 cells in the Mint. The pressure was on again.

The Mint was a filthy place. The enemy had built a pigpen in the alley around the cells to house the camp's pigs. The smell of those pigs slopping through the filth outside my window, together with the din of squealing that they made, was quite a change from the long nights of quiet conversation with George.

But being alone again was even more of a shock. I knew that (for my sanity's sake) I had to reestablish my system of discipline immediately. By May of 1967 I had developed over one hundred hymns and Scriptures by memory. Of course, they weren't perfect; in fact, back in freedom now I'm having to check them out and rememorize them correctly. But they were mine, and I had a regular program each day in my cell to go over them one by one.

My routine included rising early and charting my day. The key was to plan more tasks than I could possibly accomplish. I spent the morning pacing the cell in three steps, then turning around and pacing back again—back and forth every morning, humming quietly every hymn I knew, repeating the words, verse by verse in my mind. I had arranged the songs in groups of five. I would wind up each group with a prayer, first for my daughters Peggy and Barbara, then another group of five hymns and prayers for my oldest daughter Sondra, then five more hymns for my son John, then five more for my wife Phyllis, and then my mother, and so forth. I would quote through my Scriptures or pick a word and try to develop that word into another hymn or Scripture buried deep in my memory, waiting to be discovered.

One day I thought of the word cymbal and the phrase "sounding brass and tinkling cymbal," fell into place. Eventually I reconstructed that whole love poem in 1 Corinthians 13, but the Apostle Paul would have looked with horror at my arrangement of his masterpiece. I began with "Now abideth faith, hope and love, but the greatest of these is love," and went backwards from there through a dozen or so verses, ending with "sounding brass and tinkling cymbal." I had the whole thing totally out of order; the first verse was the last; the last, first. So, I messed up, but the thoughts were right, and often those verses sustained me.

My system was a mind-saver; but after twenty-seven days of conversation with another human being, I had to get "on the line" again. I guess I was out of practice and tapped out a message to a cell nearby before the area had been thoroughly cleared. A guard surprised me in the act, and I was punished.

He shackled me to my slab in rear cuffs and irons. For five days I couldn't move. It was summer and very hot. The humidity must have been in the 90s, the temperature in the 100s. I developed one of those severe heat rashes where the red welts turn to blisters and ultimately to boils. At first I wasn't too concerned about the boils. But they wouldn't come to a head, so I'd have to pick them to stop the swelling. I didn't know the pus was contagious or that the bug inside the poison caused the boils to spread. In a few days I counted at least sixty boils about one inch in diameter over my entire body—under my arms, in my nose, in my hair, on my ears, legs, arms, hands, and fingers.

I couldn't bathe. The water itself was crawling with filth to infect the open sores. I tried putting lye soap on the boils, but that only seemed to irritate them more.

Finally the boils got so bad I felt like Job. They began to attack my spirit. I prayed often through those miserable nights for God to heal them. I don't know why God answers some prayers with relief and others with silence. But like Job I could only go on trusting Him. The alternatives are too bleak to consider. It wasn't long until I received my second act of kindness from the enemy; a medic gave me some sulfa pills, and in a few days the boils were gone.

6

Alcatraz

In the absolute center of Hanoi, right behind the National Ministry of Defense, is a walled, island-like prison called Alcatraz. No more than 50 x 50 feet in size, this maximal security area contains only two buildings—one housing three cells; the other housing ten. Alcatraz had been a high-security prison built by the French for their VIP prisoners.

On October 25, 1967, eleven of us with reputations as POW incorrigibles were chosen by the enemy to be transported immediately to Alcatraz. We were, for the most part, senior officers who had taken active resistance roles, establishing communications and encouraging noncooperation. The North Vietnamese isolated us in the heart of their capital to put us out of circulation and to help curtail the resistance movement. We promptly nicknamed ourselves "The Alcatraz Gang."

There was Commander Jim Stockdale from Illinois, the senior ranking naval officer whose policies in Las Vegas during the summer of '67 had been so effective; and Commander Jerry Denton from Mobile, Alabama, second senior naval officer whose great leadership organized the Zoo in '66. Both men were active communicators and aggressive leaders. Commander Harry Jenkins, Washington, D.C.; Capt. Jim Mulligan, Lawrence,

Massachusetts; and I were also senior naval officers and each had resistance as reasons for our sentence.

Air Force Captain Ron Storz was there, another effective communicator from New York, who administered Jim Stockdale's policies in Las Vegas, as was Comdr. Bob Shumaker, second pilot captured in 1965, a resister who gave the enemy nothing but trouble. Then there was Air Force Capt. George McKnight, my old roommate, and Navy Lt. George Coker. Both earned their ticket for having escaped from Dirty Bird Prison in October '67. Upon recapture they were singled out for the honor of joining us at Alcatraz.

The last two men were Major Sam Johnson from Texas, a hard resister, and Lt. Commander Nels Tanner, a navy man from Tennessee. Nels had earned his ticket to Alcatraz in a press conference in Hanoi where he "confessed" with a straight face and sincere voice that there were at least two turncoat pilots in his squadron. They were Ben Casey and Clark Kent! Of course television audiences around the world immediately recognized Doctor Casey and Superman from a popular TV show and comic-page fame and laughed that propaganda bulletin to shame.

But there was nothing funny about Alcatraz. Each cell had a cement sleeping slab and a walking area no more than four feet square. There were no windows, and the small transom-like space above the solid iron door had been very neatly secured with a steel plate. At last we knew the truth about that old refrigerator joke—when the guards closed the door, the light really did go out. In the winter the cells were refrigerator cold, and in the summer they were stifling.

To make matters worse, we spent fifteen hours a day with our legs in shackles. Every night we slept in those 10- to 20-pound leg irons. In the winter they got icy-cold beneath our thin blankets, and in summer they cooked us. We were unshackled on the Tet holiday and at Christmas, but for sixteen months we wore them almost every day.

Immediately, in spite of the handicaps, we set up a communication system. Through covert communication techniques—tapping, semaphore, quick snatches of conversation, coded notes, coughs, sneezes, and the tapping broom or sliding Ho-Chi-Minh sandals—we talked to each other every day. Soon we were sharing intimate details about each other's family life, military career, and religious faith. There may have been cement and iron walls separating each man from the next, but by now we had all learned how important each man was to the other. Our circle of friendship grew strong and intimate. I think I can honestly say, the more we knew about each man's strengths or weaknesses, the more we loved each other.

The Vietnamese tried to exploit us one against the other. They tried to get us to contribute propaganda statements or tapes, and when we refused, we were punished. The interrogation room was also used for torture; and when one of us went inside, we all suffered with him. We had no secrets, and the bonds of friendship built there will last an eternity.

By now, most of us had suffered from torture and deprivation. We received almost no medicine during our entire prison terms, and because our two daily meals consisted primarily of pumpkin or cabbage soup with a few pieces of pig fat floating on the greasy surface, our protein intake was extremely low. Therefore, our resistance to disease and infection was down; we had to be extremely careful. If we stubbed a toe, we knew we would lose a toenail. Because we received little, if any, medical assistance during those long years of prison, we had to devise home remedies.

For the ever-present diarrhea, dysentery, or flu, pieces of charcoal salvaged from a dump pile might help. For skin infections or serious cuts and scratches, we washed with lye soap and bore the irritation to achieve healing. Our intestines were crawling with worms that would work their way out through our system in surprising ways. One night Harry woke up with what he thought was a piece of string in his mouth. He pulled out a six-inch worm! Now and then the enemy would throw a red pepper into our soup. We soon discovered that the pepper cleaned out worms. When no peppers were available, we tried to steal a drink of kerosene from a lantern. That quick snort of stolen kerosene fixed the worms and almost fixed the thief who had them.

We did what we could to keep each other's spirits high. One favorite method was to sweep out messages of encouragement to the entire compound with our broom. Each morning one by one we would dump our bucket in the hole near the latrine. Jerry Denton would be the last man down, and he would sweep out the latrine area, slowly using each stroke to communicate in code.

One day in 1968 we were all believing the war must end soon; the bombing had increased, and we were looking for a sign of hope. Day by day we waited, and day by day no sign came. The morale was down when Jerry went to clean that day. We listened as he tapped, "In Thy gentle hands, we are smiling our thanks!" It was a strange message but an important reminder that in spite of our hopelessness, we could be thankful. Jerry helped me remember my blessings, though small, for gratitude was the way to defeat the power of loneliness and fear. I found, even in Alcatraz, plenty to be thankful for, and it made all the difference.

During those days I worked my mind double time to stave off the temptation to lie down and die. I built five houses in my imagination during my seven years in North Vietnam. Carefully I selected the site, then negotiated with its owner for purchase. Personally, I cleared the ground, dug the foundations, laid the cement, put up the walls, shingled the roof, and landscaped the property. After I had carefully furnished the home, I sold it, took my profit, and began the entire process once again. I'll probably never build my own home in freedom, but in solitary confinement I enjoyed the mental exercise, nail by nail, and can recall today each stage of every house I built.

I also reconstructed, day by day, my childhood in Tulsa, my marriage to Phyllis, and the growth of our family. I soon realized how insensitive I had been with my family and how preoccupied I had become with my own interests. I had dropped out of church almost immediately after marriage and left my family to develop their spiritual life on their own. One memory that especially haunted me was a trip to El Paso that I made with Phyllis and the children. I was feeling guilty for paying them so little attention, and so to compensate, I offered them money to buy any Mexican merchandise they desired. I showed John the beautiful leather goods, the elaborate stone chess sets, and the colorful peasant shirts and sandals. He chose a rather amateurish sketch of Jesus in a rough wooden frame. I had offered him anything, and when he chose that rather ugly picture, I plainly showed my disappointment. Every time in prison I recalled my thoughtless, insensitive reaction, I got a knot in my stomach.

Here my young son was already showing interest in something more than baseball and routine chores. He was sending me signals loud and clear, and I missed them. How many signals I must have missed from Phyllis, Sondra, Peggy, Barbara, as well as John. I was too busy doing "other things" to really be a dad. How I regretted those late-night cocktail parties that seemed strategic to my life. I decided in Vietnam that if I were ever free again, I would try to listen, try to understand, and try to show spiritual leadership in my home and with my family.

Every day in Alcatraz I repeated my devotional routine, my prayers, Scripture quoting, and my songs. By now I could quote about 120 hymns and Scriptures. But every day it got harder to believe we would ever really be free again. It seemed the war would never end. I remember Alcatraz as a time of loneliness and misery, constant harassment, torture, and interrogation; but I

I remember Alcatraz as a time of loneliness and misery, constant harassment, torture, and interrogation.

don't remember one of the Alcatraz Gang ever losing faith in God or in his country.

Alcatraz is the source of my saddest memory of all my POW experiences. Eleven of us went in. Only ten came back. Ron Storz, the sensitive, young, air force captain from New York, was not really well upon arrival at Alcatraz; but in spite of physical weakness, he was a real leader. His message by example was "unity over self." An able, aggressive communicator, Ron loved to tap out messages with the broom. He was an Episcopalian and a sensitive Christian brother. One day in 1969 he swept through that compound a message that was perhaps the most effective sermon I have ever heard. "Seek God here! This is where you'll find Him."

Like all of us he was probably wrestling with his increasing anxiety to get out of that miserable place and into the light again. But when freedom didn't come, he reminded us all plainly to quit sulking and get down to the important business of seeking God now, rather than waiting for some better time or place.

One day Ron swept a very different kind of message. With his broom he tapped, "God, hear my cries." We all knew Ron was very ill. He was getting weaker and his weight had dropped from around 175 pounds to just over 100. He was quite emaciated, and even the enemy was growing aware of his plight. One day Frenchy, our interrogator, approached Ron in our corridor and told him he would have to move to the larger interrogation room and out of the tiny cell.

Ron argued loudly to stay with his friends. All he wanted was a roommate. After months of solitary confinement, he needed to talk to someone. The enemy had permitted Ron no letters from home and now even though they knew his mental and physical strengths were depreciating rapidly they would not give him a roommate. They tried to separate Ron from the rest of us, but Ron would not go.

Finally, Frenchy had to explain that in a few short hours his friends would be leaving Alcatraz and that he would have to remain. The Vietnamese were not hard on Ron that night. They did not make him move. All of us had heard it. Frenchy said tonight we would be moving out. After almost two years in Alcatraz, we would be leaving. That night we moved, one at a time, into a waiting truck, past Ron in his lonely cell. It was one of the hardest moments of my life as a POW. The worst part of being a prisoner is the helplessness to reach out and lift up another man in need. We couldn't even say good-by. They had the burp guns. They had the power.

War is like that for both sides. I'm sure the enemy had families who bled and died. I'm sure the enemy cried when loved ones went away and did not return. I'm sure they, too, were tempted to give way to anger and hatred. But revenge is God's business. Anger and hatred can destroy us all. When it's over, we must try to forget and to forgive.

We never stopped praying for Ron and for his family, but we knew we would probably never see him again until that day God chose to reunite the Alcatraz Gang in another world free from such pain and sorrow.

7

Stardust

As the enemy's trucks carted us away from Alcatraz that cold, winter night in December 1969 we dared to hope that the nightmare was ending and that we were going home. But when the blindfolds were removed and we were standing once again beneath the walls of the Hanoi Hilton, our hope died. The guards escorted us past New Guy Village and Heartbreak Hotel, and the iron doors of Las Vegas swung open to receive us once again.

Everything seemed the same. The place was as bleak and cold and filthy as ever. The waters of the Sands still ran thick with sewage, alive with parasites of every description. Men were still crowded into cells not big enough for animals, and the pigs still slopped in troughs around the Mint, my wretched home in '67.

I felt agony and anger as the turnkey slammed that iron door and I found myself once again in solitary confinement. This time my home was a cramped cell in Cell Block Stardust. It was like repeating a bad dream. Would it all begin again, the long interrogations, the threats, the torture? Had nothing changed?

Little by little it dawned that something had changed at Las Vegas. There were no agonizing cries in the night from torture rooms. There were no fresh rope burns, no new broken bones. Physical torture had ended, or so it seemed. The rumor spread. Hope mounted.

Soon the Cat himself confirmed our suspicions. Major Bai, chief North Vietnamese staff officer and supervisor of the various prison-camp commanders throughout Hanoi, told Jerry Denton and me that prisoners would no longer suffer physical torture and abuse. Speaking quietly and in broken English, his former cocky manner subdued, his spirit broken, the Cat explained the reason.

"I have misinterpreted the will of the Vietnamese people," he told us. "For four thousand years the policy of the people has been humane and lenient treatment toward prisoners. I have misread and misinterpreted the party's will. I have gone before the people and confessed." Soon after his strange confession, Major Bai disappeared from the Hoa Lo prison complex, and, to my knowledge, he has not been seen again.

Was the Cat speaking truth? Would the torture end? Why had the policy been changed? With growing excitement, the questions raced through our minds. We didn't know about the volunteer organizations in America that were working so hard through bracelets and bumper stickers to keep our plight before the public. We hadn't heard about the strenuous efforts on our behalf by the world's leaders, the International Red Cross, and patriotic organizations all across our country. We couldn't know about the thousands of letters and cables the North Vietnamese were receiving from the little people all around the world. We only knew that the Cat had spoken to a few of us, and the word needed to be spread.

However, most senior officers were still living in solitary confinement, and it would be no small task to get such news spread quickly and convincingly from our cell block to other cell blocks within the Hanoi Hilton and throughout Hanoi to the other prisons: the Plantation, the Son Tay Camps Faith and Hope, and the Zoo. But to get the word out was imperative, because the enemy was still using threats of torture and coercion to get us to submit and to cooperate in its propaganda campaign.

Alan Paton once wrote in his *Cry the Beloved Country* that men are held "by chains of fear and fear of chains." We had to put the prisoners' minds at rest. We didn't need to fear. Resistance would not be met with torture. Fortunately, the Alcatraz Gang had gone to work immediately to establish lines of communication, and it wasn't long until the word was out.

The Asian flu was spreading through Hanoi about this time, and at least 75 to 80 percent of the prisoners in the camp came down with high fever and dysentery. For three days I couldn't move off my plank bed. Then, just as I was getting strong enough to sit up and stare another bowl of rotten-cabbage soup in the face, a guard opened my door, and in walked Harry Jenkins. It was Wednesday night, February 25, 1970, and during more than four years of captivity, I had lived outside of solitary confinement for only twenty-seven wonderful days with George Mc-Knight. During all my years in prison, I had not been more than thirty feet away from Commander Jenkins, and we knew each other intimately through our covert communication efforts. But after four years, to shake his hand and know that when the turnkey walked away, I would be face-to-face with another human being—and not alone—was something else!

We talked nonstop for several days and nights. It may have been in whispers, but the sound of our voices was like music. Sometimes we would go for years without using our voices in prison. Several times I honestly was afraid that when I tried to speak again, nothing would happen. But during those next thirty days with Jenkins it happened around the clock. Even with the thousands of words we got off during those first days, few were wasted. Fighting doesn't end because a man's plane is shot down or his squad is captured. The war isn't over for a man thrown into a high security, escape-proof prison. The prisoner of war works round the clock to beat the enemy, and Harry and I had much to accomplish in the short time we had together.

A prisoner in the Desert Inn cell block in Las Vegas was hav-

I followed last, lagging behind just long enough to whisper the code.

ing trouble getting "on the line." He didn't know the code and needed tutoring; this was our chance to teach him letter by letter how to communicate. Fortunately Waldo, one of our regular camp guards, was not too bright. With Waldo's help we could get the new man "on the line" and mend the broken communications link.

The plan was simple. On our daily walks to the latrine dumping area, Harry would try walking so close to Waldo that the poor, unsuspecting guard would never see me lagging back just long enough to whisper the code, bit by bit, to the new man in Desert Inn.

It worked! The sight must have caused a lot of stifled laughter to any prisoner who might have been watching this charade through transom slit or barred window. First came Waldo, shuffling along, mumbling to himself. Then Harry followed, literally tripping over Waldo's heels, clicking our honey pots together now and then, and making sufficient heavy breathing and noisy footsteps for the two of us. I followed last, lagging behind just long enough to whisper the code, then running madly to catch up before Waldo got the wiser. He never suspected a thing, and in a matter of days the new man was "on the line."

We assigned ourselves, or were assigned, important tasks to accomplish every day. Surveillance of the camp area became an art form. We determined to know the perimeters of each prison with considerable more detail than the enemy knew them. Every POW's trip to an interrogation room became a mission to sight, memorize, and report back on specific areas of the prison. We knew every rusty nail that might support a rope or wire. We knew which windows were barred and which were large enough for a man to crawl through. We knew the location of every cell, cell block, guard post, administration building, even the immediate area outside the walls.

Although escape was always in the back of our minds, it wasn't the primary goal of disciplined surveillance. Knowing the intricate details of the prisons had practical day-by-day importance for survival. For example, in July of '66 a new guy, Lt. Commander Cole Black, a neighbor of mine in San Diego, was spotted through a crack in the door in a cell in the Zoo. No one knew that he was down, yet somehow the enemy had him. He wasn't "on the line," didn't know the code. We had to get it to him.

On an earlier surveillance trip, a fellow prisoner had noticed that a clothesline was attached to one end of the new man's cell. Prisoners hanging clothes could whisper the code to Commander Black in segments until he knew it all. From that moment a lot of prisoners used filthy water to wash clothes that would have been better off dirty so that piece by piece the new guy could learn the code and get "on the line." The effort required elaborate preparation and coordination by three different cells, but once again surveillance paid off.

By the time we left that vile prison complex, I could sit down and draw an intricate, detailed description of the entire prison, many sections of which I had never even seen. Surveillance and covert communication helped defeat the enemy's painstaking effort to keep us isolated, confined, and hidden. Isolation is a terrible weapon. Strong men have been destroyed by it. I was constantly amazed at how the loneliness could break my own willingness to resist. Physical torture may have ended, but there is still no torture worse than years of solitary confinement. Our successful struggle to communicate with each other turned a group of prisoners, isolated by cement and steel walls, into a community, and through that community we survived.

Harry Jenkins and I were separated four months later. I spent the last six months of 1970 living alone again. The days after one loses a friend are the hardest days to bear. Immediately I had to develop all kinds of new mental projects to fill those lonely hours. I worked for months trying to recall the names and faces of every member of my high-school graduating class. While try-

ing to remember faces forgotten twenty-four years, I was reminded again how generous God has been in giving man wonderful and mysterious powers.

At night, exhausted from my mental search for high-school
friends and asleep at last, I would suddenly awaken with a new
name or face recalled. While my body slept, my brain worked
on. This computerlike miracle between our ears seems so strong
a proof of a loving Father behind creation. In spite of my problems in prison, it became easier to thank God for His gifts. It
almost seemed that the less possessions I had, the more signifi-
cant His really worthwhile gifts became to me.

We didn't have much in the way of possessions during those
first five years in prison—a blanket, a pajamalike prison suit, a
drinking cup, a honey bucket, and a mosquito net. We had no
books, no Bible (every New Year's Eve for seven years, I repeated my resolution that after my release I would never be
without a Bible again), no newspapers. (In fact, I didn't learn
that Neil Armstrong had walked on the moon until three years
after his return!) We missed pencils and notebooks, and radios
and soft pillows, but most of all, I think, we missed decent food
—let alone home cooking. Our food was basically the same
those first five years. We ate two meals a day. It was either rice
or hard French bread with a liter of boiled water. Also, we had
a bowl of soup, the rotten cabbage or seaweed varieties, and in
the summer sewer greens, little green shoots that grew around
sewers. These were thrown on top of the soup, with a piece or
two of sowbelly—all fat—plus skin and hair. We didn't eat very
high off the hog; you can believe that! Now and then we would
get a fish head or tail, all scrap, maybe a hamster, and, if lucky,
dog meat or fragged duck. (The men called it "fragged duck"
because the duck had been cleavered—bones and all—into tiny
fragments.)

Most of what we ate I considered inedible before prison, but
meat—even dog meat—is the prime source of protein, and to sur-

vive we ate it, hair and all. On special days the enemy might prepare a very edible meal. Usually photographers would be on hand to use our enjoyment of the meal as propaganda, but we all gave in and ate gratefully. On rare occasions a package from home would get through. Everyone would share this unexpected bonanza. If a man got a bottle of vitamins, everyone in camp would get a vitamin that day until the bottle was empty. Our motto was UNITY BEFORE SELF. We shared and in the sharing kept each other alive.

It's important to remember that the North Vietnamese are terribly poor people. Our bombing and blockades had cut down all supplies, including foodstuff; and though we suffered extraordinarily, we weren't the only ones who went to bed hungry in that land.

I lost more than forty pounds in captivity, and I was skinny when captured. The last two years the food increased in quality and quantity. I gained back twenty pounds primarily because the enemy initiated a third meal—the Vietnamese version of breakfast—a cup of hot powdered milk or sugar and a piece of bread. If the war had ended three years earlier, you would have seen a different crew of survivors—skinnier, leaner, and meaner perhaps. That added breakfast those last few years did a lot to mellow us and to fatten us for release.

Perhaps the greatest boost to our morale came during the last few weeks in Stardust. November 21, 1970, the prison and its immediate environs exploded into activity—trucks, troops, and tanks moving in all directions. We saw lights in the night and new construction in the prison. By the evening of November 24, more than two hundred downed American air crews had moved into the western section of the Hanoi Hilton, trucked there blindfolded from camps all around Hanoi.

Finally, we learned what happened that historic night, November 21, 1970. Colonel Bull Simons and his group of seventy had invaded North Vietnam in jet-powered helicopters to search out and rescue prisoners. They landed in the area of Son Tay, about fifteen miles west of Hanoi, and besieged a POW camp there. Unfortunately, at that time there were no Americans being held in that area; but when the word got out that such a mission had taken place, we had concrete evidence that we were not forgotten—that our nation was really trying to bring us home. After that invasion things were never the same at the Hanoi Hilton.

8

Camp Unity

Pacing my 4 x 8 foot cell in Cell Block Stardust at the Hanoi Hilton, my mind busy recalling a verse of some forgotten hymn, I suddenly remembered this was Christmas Day. My memory flashed to our home in San Diego at Christmas. It had been six years since our family had gathered together around a tree loaded with gifts for a day of food and fun. I pictured Phyllis carrying the Christmas turkey to our table and ten-year-old John jumping up and down, begging to carve it. My daughters Sondra, Peggy, and Barbara, looking beautiful and proud, had set the table in our Christmas finest. How we had enjoyed those feasts together! Earlier that day the children had torn into our endless pile of presents, heaping the torn wrappings into a growing pile, squealing with feigned surprise over gifts they had spied out earlier, hidden in closets and underneath their parents' bed.

Six years had passed since our family had been together around the Christmas tree, and my eyes filled with tears prompted by those happy memories; but in my cell that day, I was astounded to realize how unaware I had been of the real meaning of Christmas on those days so long ago. Oh, I knew it was Christ's birthday and I knew He was God's Son—Someone very special. That was nice, but it took prison to help me to see what Christmas really meant. All the world was a prison, and every man a prisoner until He came. On that night two thousand years ago, God had invaded my world. Like Colonel Bull Simons and his brave group of seventy, God came down to search out and rescue prisoners. Baby Jesus, lying in a filthy manger, surrounded by the smells and sounds of the barnyard, was more than a cute, cuddly kid, as Christmas cards portray Him. He was God Himself come down. He would grow to manhood. He would risk His life to break open prison doors. He would die to set men free. Christmas Day would be the beginning of freedom for men who would believe. I spent that day thinking of the freedom I felt in Christ and wishing to be free to celebrate His birth again with my family.

That Christmas night my devotional reveries were disturbed by the sounds of guards entering Las Vegas, throwing open cellblock doors. Without warning all of us in Las Vegas were herded one-by-one out of that stinking place and into one large area we promptly dubbed Camp Unity. Talk about a celebration! We laughed and hugged and chatted excitedly. We had no idea why we were together or what it meant—but we were together. And if it were only for a night, we would enjoy it.

Up to that point I had spent fifty-eight months in solitary confinement with only a few short breaks; that is 1,740 days alone. Other men had spent over four years in solitary, too; and here we were, milling about in a big room, shaking hands with men we had known and loved for years—men we knew intimately, yet had never seen. For years it had taken as much as twenty-four hours to get a message around that crowd and twenty-four hours to get the answer back. Men had risked and suffered much to communicate a sentence in a day. Now, suddenly, we were face-to-face. Everybody wanted to talk to everybody else simultaneously. It was a wild and happy Christmas night.

Here we were milling about in a big room, shaking hands with men we had known and loved for years.

The enemy had gathered all the downed American aircrews into this one prison. There were nine cell blocks around Camp Unity. Each of them had about forty men. One of the first things we did in Camp Unity was to begin regular church services in every cell block. In the past five years we had sent covert devotional messages from cell to cell, but now we would sit down and worship together in groups. We sang a hymn, someone quoted Scripture, another prayed, a third man shared a meditation. Everything was from memory. There were no hymnbooks, no Bibles, no pews. The service was imperfect but beautiful and very important to our morale. Almost every prisoner entered into worship wholeheartedly.

The enemy immediately decided that church services would be interrupted and the worshipers disbanded. To the North Vietnamese, most of whom didn't speak our language, this was a political meeting. Asians, friends and foes alike, use singing and speeches in group gatherings like our church services for political purposes. Our service was immediately suspected of being a dangerous rallying point. Of course, we tried to explain that we had assembled simply to worship God. We even invited the English-speaking enemy officers to join us in our service so that they would convince our guards that this was church and nothing else. They refused.

The pressure to discontinue worship mounted. Though the torture had ended, threats were made. Reprisals were promised. The guards would heckle us, trying to drown out the words of those who led—but we refused to give up our right to worship God. It seemed the most natural and proper issue on which to take our stand. We enjoyed this new taste of communal life, but we would risk the privilege to keep our right to worship together. A showdown was inevitable.

The cell blocks in Camp Unity were divided more or less by seniority. I was in the senior cell block during that first wonderful month of communal living. We knew that if the enemy had to be confronted with our right to hold church services on Sunday morning, that confrontation would be our task. So, for two weeks we invited the Vietnamese (those who spoke English and their officers) to join us in church to see what we were doing and to prove we were doing nothing to endanger the internal security of their prison. They continued to refuse, and by the third Sunday the confrontation was imminent.

February 7, 1971, all the guards in camp hung around the senior cell block. This was it. George Coker, the young navy lieutenant from Alcatraz, was acting as the chaplain in our cell block that Sunday. He was the junior officer in the building, yet it was his morning to conduct the service and address the group. We had a small choir to sing a familiar hymn. I was going to recite the 101st Psalm, and Lt. Colonel Risner was going to lead the benediction.

As we began the morning's hymn, the doors opened, and the guards poured in. We had already decided to continue the worship at any cost, and we all looked straight at Lieutenant Coker as he spoke. The guards tried to keep him quiet. They argued and cursed angrily; Lieutenant Coker just kept talking.

Then it was my turn. The guards tried to interfere in every way they could short of physical abuse. I continued quoting Psalm 101; they kept yelling for me to stop. The choir sang and Lt. Colonel Risner gave the benediction prayer. By now the guards were embarrassed and angry and determined to have revenge.

The service ended, but no one moved except the guards who stalked out angrily. The "church riot" had been heard by everyone, and we all waited for the ax to fall. Fifteen minutes passed before the guards returned. Then they reentered Cell Block 7 and called out Lieutenant Coker, Lt. Colonel Risner, and myself; the three of us were herded into the courtyard just outside the cell-block gate.

Everyone watched as we nervously awaited our fate. I must

confess the memories of past torture and abuse were still vivid in my mind. What did the enemy have planned? What would that short service cost us?

As we stood, each alone with his own questions, each handling his own anxieties, a fantastic thing happened. Somewhere in Cell Block 7 someone began to sing the first verse of "The Star-Spangled Banner." It had not been sung (on penalty of severe punishment) for five long years, but somewhere, someone was singing it. Others joined in. Before one line had passed, all of Cell Block 7 was alive with that song; and by the time the officer returned to march us away, it seemed that every cell block in Camp Unity was singing.

O say, can you see, by the dawn's early light,
What so proudly we hailed at the twilight's last gleaming,
Whose broad stripes and bright stars, through the perilous fight,
O'er the ramparts we watched were so gallantly streaming?
And the rockets' red glare, the bombs bursting in air,
Gave proof through the night that our flag was still there;
O say, does that Star-Spangled Banner yet wave
O'er the land of the free and the home of the brave?

There was a lump in my throat as we were marched away from our friends, the sounds of the national anthem ringing through that old French prison in Hanoi. Of course, we had no idea where we were going or what we would find when we got there. So that march and the months that followed were torturous. Alone again after a taste of communal living, locked in Heartbreak-sized small cells, forced to communicate covertly again was torture, indeed. But we had conquered! From that Sunday until the prisoners were released, church services were held throughout the prison with little, if any, interference from the enemy.

Junior officers remained in communal-living status for the rest of their imprisonment, but the senior officers were eventually locked into what we called Building Zero. When Lt. Colonel Risner and I arrived in Zero, we found small cells, appalling filth, and extreme heat. At least ten men were in irons; sometimes two on a bunk. They weren't permitted out and had to perform all their bodily functions with their legs shackled to the slab. Lt. Colonel Risner and I were not in irons, so we set about to clear the guards, begin communications, and raise the spirits of the men who suffered there.

Here in Building Zero—code name Rawhide—I talked for the first time through closed doors to Col. John Flynn, the senior prisoner in North Vietnam. John is an extremely strong yet sensitive man and proved an outstanding leader. He had been informed of the church riot in Cell Block 7 and had decided for us to have church in Building Zero. Remember, Rawhide imprisoned men in cells, isolated from each other, shackled in solitary or small groups; but Colonel Flynn knew how much even a brief time of prayer and worship would mean.

We plotted carefully to clear the area and conduct the service. Robby Risner prayed a magnificent prayer, and I quoted imperfectly but with enthusiasm, the 101st Psalm; Jack Finley, an air force lieutenant colonel, whistled "Ave Maria." I don't remember hearing anything so beautiful in my life as Jack's version of that great old Catholic song. We worshiped regularly in Rawhide in spite of barriers of brick and cement; in fact, we even formed a choir with individual members separated by their cells. Those men could really sing. We were all denominations. All the things that could have divided us didn't matter in Building Zero. We were united in our faith in God and in each other. Nothing else mattered.

March 19, 1971, I moved into a 6 x 7 foot cell with my old and great friends Harry Jenkins, Jim Stockdale, and Jerry Denton. There were only two concrete bunks, no ventilation, no windows; we were four men locked together in a room with little or no space to walk; it was hot and filthy and crowded. Each of us carefully organized his daily schedule, trying to be sensitive to each other without giving up the discipline, physical and mental, long established. It was easy to be irritable. None of us had any saintly inclinations. There were harsh words and embarrassing silences, but we were united against a common enemy. The enemy was more than ignorant and abusive guards. The enemy was loneliness and fear and death. We would survive, and we would survive with honor. Any anger or impatience between us quickly dissolved in our common task—to survive— and in our love for one another.

I never stopped doing my daily routines. Some part of each day was filled with Scripture recall. We worked together to find more. Every man found some floating in his memory and contributed to the pile. Daily I would pray for my family, and renew my resolve to make my commitment to Christ, and join my family's church upon return to freedom. In prison I firmly believed that there was a God who loved me and was working in my life. I cannot explain with reason or proof why my faith was central to my survival. But it was. Other men went in unbelieving and came out the same. I didn't, and for me my faith in Christ made all the difference.

Somehow we all survived that long hot summer of '71, and in September, nine of us were moved into Cell Block 8. These were the nine senior officers under Colonel Flynn. We had already organized the cell blocks into a complete, sophisticated command structure much like an air force wing command, with Colonel Flynn as the wing commander. Every building in our covert communications system was given a code name. If the enemy intercepted our traffic, he had no idea what it meant, who originated it, or who was to receive the message. Cell Block 8 became our headquarters. We gave it code name BLUE. The wing commander's code was SKY. So any man who received a message from SKY BLUE knew that Wing Commander Flynn was sending it from headquarters.

My responsibility as wing communications officer was to keep communications open, to keep every man "on the line." If we could keep every man alert and informed, he would not fall to angry interrogators pushing for propaganda statements or military information. When one man went to interrogation, we all knew immediately and sent waves of support in his direction. We were working at maximal resistance and had one united goal: **RELEASE WITH HONOR.** We wanted to leave that place as men, standing tall and proud, not broken and bent. Our goal was to produce men who had more than survived—men who had conquered.

Besides promoting mental activity, the wing worked to get us back in good physical health. Every man ate everything he could. Exercise programs were part of the wing's organization, and even those men with broken bones worked hard to get and keep their bodies in shape. Cellmates would walk their rooms for miles a day in line, do push-ups, sit-ups, and run in place. The organization worked to get us ready for that day we hoped lay ahead— *Freedom!*

Remember, all our communications were still covert. It took time and effort. The enemy knew of this underground wing organization and did everything short of physical torture to chop communications and kill our system. But the enemy could not stop us. It was a great and exciting effort on the part of many men that kept our wing command strong and effective during those last long months of imprisonment.

Moving then, in September of '71, was a big move up for all of us. It was the first time in six years that I had been in a cell with an open window—there were bars, but it was a window. It wasn't dark in that cell, and now and then breezes made breathing bearable. In fact, often in the daytime we were allowed into a small

12 x 12 foot courtyard area for two or three hours a day; for the first time in 75 months I felt the sunshine on my face. The walls around me were 15 feet high and broken glass was imbedded in their surface, but I could look up past those walls and see the sun. It was a glorious sight.

We even had a kind of Vietnamese toilet. It was only a hole with a squatting place, but it was a luxury. I still dreamed of beautiful white toilet seats, white pillow cases, a soft bed with clean sheets, and chocolate-covered peanuts! We weren't home yet, and the conditions, though improved, were still frightful by any standards. There were still the mosquitoes, the insects, the lice, the parasites that lived on and in our bodies, and the rats that surprised us by nibbling on our toes at night.

As I was stretched out on my hardwood bed in Cell Block 8 one night, I was awakened by the feeling that something was gnawing on the end of my thumb. It was a rat the size of a small opossum; and when I yelled, I scared him as much as he had scared me. Unfortunately, we were both trapped in my mosquito net. We rolled together biting and bashing, but with the help of my cellmates, I finally did him in. Those experiences look funny to me now. They didn't then!

My friends in prison had all been Americans until Cell Block 8. There I met three outstanding men from Thailand and one South Vietnamese pilot, allies shot down, captured, and imprisoned like ourselves. The South Vietnamese could speak English, French, Spanish and Thai. He was a brilliant young man, an able friend and conspirator against the enemy. The Thais were industrious and friendly, but they couldn't speak English, so at first we couldn't communicate. I must confess at first we were suspicious of them because we didn't know who or what they were. As trustees who worked around the compound, they had access to all our secrets. We watched and waited and wondered if they were friends or foes. Then one day the South Vietnamese pilot spoke out.

"Commander, do you trust me?" he asked through the wall that separated us.

I didn't hesitate. "Of course, I trust you. We are allies. You were shot down fighting with us. Why shouldn't I trust you?"

He paused and then continued. "If you trust me," he said, "know this; the three Thais are true and loyal friends. You must trust them too."

That ended the matter, and immediately we set about teaching the Thais English and the code. They learned them both, and we were constantly amazed and grateful for their skills and friendship. We always ended our communications in code throughout the wing sending R.W.H.S.W.D.G.B.U!, which translates: RE-LEASE WITH HONOR. STICK WITH DICK. GOD BLESS YOU!

The Thais were Buddhists, and I was surprised to get a message one day that ended with the part of that sign-off that they could not really understand: GOD BLESS YOU! On Christmas and Easter I had spent time tapping out the meaning of these holidays. Perhaps they had understood.

We worked hard those last months of 1972, contacting new people, maintaining our organization, and operating covertly inside of the Hoa Lo prison complex. People may wonder why we didn't attempt escape. Unfortunately, they believe that prison life is like the world of "Hogan's Heroes," that slapstick television series featuring imaginary American prisoners in World War II.

There had been at least two attempts by Americans to escape from North Vietnamese prisons. George McKnight and Lieutenant Coker earned their way to Alcatraz through their escape from Dirty Bird, October 1, 1967. Ed Atterberry and John Dramesi escaped from the Zoo, May 10, 1969, but were recaptured shortly and brought back to that prison in the same truck. There they shook hands, wished each other luck and were parted. No one has ever seen Ed Atterberry again.

There were heavy reprisals for escape attempts; and though we thought about it, diagrammed the area, and made various plans in '71 and '72, our plans were never tried. We were locked in cells, inside of cell blocks, inside of a series of jagged glass and hot-wire walls, in a massive prison with inner and outer walls, with twenty-four-hour guard surveillance, in the heart of the capital city. Even if a prisoner survived an escape he would have no friends and no place to hide in downtown Hanoi. So, until 1973 we waited for the miracle of freedom to happen from the outside. One day we would be taken through the gates of the Hanoi Hilton to freedom or to death. Until that day we had to pray and work and wait.

9

Gia Lam Airport, Hanoi

On January 31, 1973, it seemed our prayers for freedom had been answered. Still living in Cell Block 8, we had learned of the agreement signed in Paris on January 28. As an important part of that agreement, the United States had demanded that the North Vietnamese deliver into prisoner hands a copy of the protocol describing our release. When we heard the news, Colonel Flynn asked the nine of us to stop our work so that we could thank God for His mercy. We had hoped and prayed for so long; now freedom was in sight. We didn't say much. I suppose we didn't have to. A look of relief and joy was on everybody's face. I am sure the good Lord could look into our hearts and see the gratitude that was there as we prayed.

I had never prayed much after dropping out of church twenty years before—never with Phyllis. But in prison many of my most important memories are associated with prayer. There were frightening prayers; for example, the prayer of thanks I whispered dangling one thousand feet over enemy land just after my jet exploded only yards before me and only moments before I was captured. There were dramatic prayers like the one Colonel Risner prayed, with the enemy cursing and yelling at him during the church riot of '71. There were prayers of great sadness like those prayers we prayed for our comrade dying and alone in Alcatraz. There were even funny prayers. One example I recall occurred in Cell Block 7. We were digging a hole between two cell blocks to help us communicate by voice between them; unfortunately the hole had to be dug with the diggers lying in the latrine. The smell was terrible. One day at grace John Dramesi prayed, "God, help them get that hole dug through the latrine before it's my turn to dig again." Talking to God became a natural process, like eating and breathing.

There were eloquent prayers by men like Commander Chuck Gillespie or Col. Norman Gaddis or Col. Dave Winn who were strong Christians and who had obviously developed seasoned prayer lives, but praying was a new experience for me. I'm still not very good at it. Words don't come easy when I pray. But even we amateurs discovered in prison the incredibly powerful force prayer can be in our lives. I learned I could talk to God anyplace, dangling from a parachute or shackled in a cesspool. I learned He could hear me whether in worship with a crowd of men or alone in solitary confinement. I learned He understood even if I fumbled the words, spoke with rotten grammar, or asked Him to do crazy, unreasonable things.

There was a time when I might have thought that men who prayed a lot were milquetoasts or sissy types. Now I know differently. There were times I thought prayer was a silly ritual we did from guilt or pressure, an act of piety we performed in church, or family worship that really didn't have much meaning. Now I know the truth. Prayer really works! I still don't pray aloud very well. But I have tested prayer and found God hears and answers. So when Colonel Flynn, the senior officer in Vietnam, asked us to stop and pray, it seemed the right and natural thing to do.

February 6, 1973, we were moved together into a large room in Cell Block 6. It was there I met for the first time since our capture Denny Moore, a man from my old squadron, who had been shot down exactly one month before I was. I thought he was dead until I learned he was being held in a cell block next to mine. To walk up to Denny and say, "Hello! Glad you are alive," to shake hands again with old friends separated for years by iron and cement was a real thrill.

We enjoyed a lot of things about Cell Block 6. I played my first volleyball game in seven years in prison; I spent wonderful hours in long conversations with old and new friends, and we had great spiritual experiences there. We gathered for worship. Howie Dunn, a marine lieutenant colonel, led a five- or six-man choir that was terrific (by now choirs were common to all the cell blocks, and on an average Sunday one could hear hymns of praise echoing through that entire prison complex).

Norm McDaniels, a very profound and sincere, black air force officer, led the worship and preached the morning meditation. He had been in a cell block where a Bible had been available for a short time, and he quoted a psalm. Then he spoke to each of us. We knew this might be our last service in prison. His subject was right on target. Being a pilot himself, he knew that none of us had ever gone into combat thinking we would be shot down, captured and imprisoned, certainly not for seven long years. Now that release was in sight, he knew we all were asking, "Why me?" He listed the reasons many of us had already been thinking. "Am I here because I have committed some ugly sin and God is punishing me for it?" "Am I here as a test of faith, a trial by fire?" "Or is it all a mistake? I accidentally got in the way of enemy fire and now God's helping me make the best of it." Each of us had to come to terms with these questions.

As I looked into my own life, I thought, "Yes, I was a sinner," and, "Yes, this has been a test of my faith," and, "Yes, God has really helped to bring something to me from those long prison years." After all, I was shot down, a church dropout, disinterested in Christian truth. I would return to freedom aware of God and anxious to stay "on the line" with Him.

Earlier in the service we had sung the Doxology.

Praise God from whom all blessings flow;
Praise Him, all creatures here below;
Praise Him above, ye heavenly host;
Praise Father, Son, and Holy Ghost.

Norm McDaniels ended his closing prayer; the choir sang the benediction hymn:

Hear our prayer, O Lord,
Hear our prayer, O Lord,
Incline Thine ear to us,
And grant us Thy peace.

Sunday, February 11, 1973, was the end of the two-week period outlined in the protocol we had received. We arose that morning wondering if this might be the day. That afternoon the North Vietnamese chopped up eight turkeys and fed them to the 200 airmen in that prison. Having turkey was not common to everyday life. Our excitement mounted.

At sunset the guards entered our cell blocks and took us, six or seven at a time, to Heartbreak. There was a moment of fear as the first group entered that ugly place filled with so many terrible memories, but quickly our spirits soared as we were issued new clothing for release. There were 115 of us chosen for this first increment, and now we had our clothing ready and our release bags packed. Sitting around that night, unable to sleep, we felt the next day to be almost anticlimactic.

We were going to leave as we had come—*with dignity*. We would go home with honor! The torture had ended; we had kept the faith. Finally, the sun rose above Hanoi. No gong was needed to get that crew of excited airmen up and dressed for this occasion. We were going home!

By 8 A.M. we were lined up outside our cells. A guard checked off our names, and we walked out of the gates of the Hanoi Hil-

ton. There were six buses waiting. We watched and waited as the
men on stretchers were loaded and driven away towards Gia Lam
Airport. Then the rest of us, less ill, wounds almost healed,
climbed on board with heads high. It was the first time in seven
years that I had sat in a vehicle without my hands in rear cuffs
and my eyes blindfolded. I watched the prison through my window as we pulled away. It had been a kind of tomb for seven
years, and now I felt resurrected from the dead, driving away to
life again.

Hanoi was in ruins. It is a poverty-stricken place—hard to describe. Long years of war had taken an effective toll. The city was
a mess, but the streets were alive with people. Apparently the
news of our release had been broadcast over Radio Hanoi. The
people lined the streets, stopped their work, and watched as we
drove by. There were many friendly gestures and happy waves.
Everyone was smiling, obviously aware of our great joy. We
didn't smile back.

When we arrived at the airport, we didn't feel particularly joy-
ful. There were no airplanes. The airport was bombed and gutted.
On one of the few buildings that remained, a Red Cross flag was
flying—the first we had seen in seven years. We unloaded the
buses. Our guards told us that there would be a delay as both
sides hammered out the final details of the turnover.

We stood around nervously. At first there were feeble attempts
at joking about our predicament. Then we lapsed into silence.
About noon the Vietnamese brought us something to drink and
some stale sandwiches. We ate them, hoping this was our last
meal in Vietnam. No one wanted any trouble. There was too
much to lose. We wanted the release to go smoothly. Others were
still in prison and our actions could affect their release.

We could see the international control teams scurrying around.
There was nothing to do but wait. Suddenly the guards loaded
us back on the buses and we drove towards loading ramps on the
runway. A cheer went up as the first C-141 transport broke

We saluted the air force colonel standing there.

through the overcast and landed. By now each of us calculated in his mind how many men per plane and which plane we would pull. It was obvious that I would be on the second C-141. It had not appeared, and as the first plane was loaded, I just knew there would be no second plane—that I would end up driving back through Hanoi to spend more time in prison.

Then the second C-141 broke through the haze and made its final approach. Suddenly the pilot added power and went back up again. I knew perfectly well this wasn't some new form of torture, but oh, how it hurt to see that plane fly by! We sweated his second approach inch by inch; and when he was finally down, we allowed ourselves a cheer. We knew now that in minutes our nightmare would be over.

The first C-141 taxied out and took off toward Clark Air Force Base in the Philippines. Then it was our turn. An especially hated North Vietnamese officer—nicknamed Slick or Soft Soap Ferry—came to our bus with a binder containing a list of names. He was one of the most dangerous men I had ever seen, known as a consummate liar and an extortioner, guilty of torture and death, and personally responsible for a great deal of our misery. There he was, calling out names. I am sure every man that crossed the line to freedom felt a flash of bitterness as Slick called each name.

Then we were walking towards the ramp. We saluted the air force colonel standing there, and one by one we were escorted to the plane. I shivered when I finally stood inside that beautiful rescue ship. Harry Jenkins and I chose the last seat in the plane and slumped gratefully into its cushions for the long ride home.

10

San Diego

A few hours in an airplane can seem an eternity to a prisoner homeward bound. Fortunately, the first hours were filled with pleasant new sights and sounds on the C-141 that carried us. This was a medic plane, and it was manned inside by a couple of beautiful American flight nurses. We hadn't seen American women for more than seven years. I must confess that all of us, including me, just stared at them with delight as they arranged our pillows and plied us with creature comforts. Their bright smiles and sweet smells after seven years of living in an all-male prison, with the smell of death in the air, were almost too much to bear.

Early in the flight we flew over the attack carrier *Enterprise* on maneuvers in the South China Sea. An old friend, Jack Christianson, was the carrier division commander now just a few thousand feet below. There was a moment of silence as we passed that beautiful ship. There wasn't a man aboard our plane who wouldn't have given his right arm to be down there operating that great carrier. All of us were professionals, and it felt so good to be back in our own world of ships and planes and pilots.

The sleek new C-141 that was carrying us provided another source of inspiration and conversation for a bunch of old flyers who had almost lost touch with their profession—in my case, for the last seven years. In fact, the airplane, the pilot and copilot had all been commissioned after I was shot down. The copilot wasn't even in high school when I was taken captive and here he was the one chosen to fly us home! I felt a bit like Rip Van Winkle waking up in the middle of an unfamiliar world. While I had been locked away in a concrete prison cell, the world had changed. My children had grown up, graduated, married, had children of their own, and I had missed it all. Men had gone to school, won their wings, flown their missions and been given commands while I had paced beneath a prison wall. It wasn't long before the cheering and the celebrating died down, and we were left alone with our memories and our questions.

What would we face at home? Who had died? Who had gone away? Men thought of wives, sweethearts, friends, parents. Many were flying home to face divorce or death in their families. Others would require extensive hospitalization; some needed surgery. There were broken bones to be reset, teeth that needed care. Many needed counseling. We all needed rest. What tragic surprises would greet us? Could we face the coming days? Could we begin again?

What would we face in America? We had heard about the antiwar activities, the demonstrations, and marches. I felt some anger at those who had opposed the war; but I had been fighting to defend their right to oppose it. But how would they feel about me now? Would we be booed in the streets? Would our families be humiliated, our children scorned? We had no idea of what our reception would be.

It was a long flight home, but all too soon it ended. The wheels touched down on the runways of Clark Air Force Base, the Philippines. We had no idea of the reception that awaited us.

Harry and I hung back as the men deplaned. I was the last one to leave the C-141, and imagine my surprise at our reception. There was a long red carpet, a clear sign of welcome known

It wasn't long before the cheering and the celebrating died down, and we were left alone with our memories and our questions.

round the world. At the head of that carpet stood Admiral Noel Gayler, Commander in Chief of the Pacific. If we had had any fears about our reception, they ended in that bus ride to Clark Hospital. The road was lined with children and adults. They carried hand-painted signs: WELCOME HOME! GOD BLESS YOU! YOU HAVE KEPT THE FAITH! It seems like a dream now—the friendly smiles—the children waving, held high on Father's shoulders—women crying—and young people cheering.

We arrived at the hospital at dinnertime and immediately got in line. The men who had arrived on the first flight were standing in hospital pajamas and wearing LIGHT DIET tags pinned to their shirts. They were glumly receiving their bowls of soup, jello, and custard when we stepped up to order steaks, and pie, and banana splits. The flawless planning of Operation Homecoming had included special diets for us all. But we had not received our tags, and needless to say, the medical officer saw that all of us could stand the shock of good American cooking, so he tore up the light diet order and we all dug in.

For three days we remained at Clark Air Force Base, and I suspect my total amount of sleep was less than three hours in that entire period. It was time to be debriefed. The names and serial numbers we had memorized were taken down by debriefing officers and compared, one list against the other. If there were men still in prison and not on the lists, our government was determined to find them. They wanted to know everything we knew about how many Americans were still in prison. What was their condition? Who were missing? Who had died?

At last I was alone in my hospital room, and the operator on my bedside phone informed me that my call to America and my family was ready. I had received only four cards of the hundreds of letters and packages she had mailed. I had waited six years before I received that first seven-line card the enemy finally granted me. Phyllis was on the line seven thousand miles away. What would she say? How would she feel about me?

"Hello, Phyllis?"

That warm voice of the woman I love, with her slight Oklahoma drawl, was full of love and welcome. She tried to put my mind at ease that everyone was well and waiting anxiously for my return. But I could sense she was holding back. Finally, she told me of my son John's accident four years before. He had been swimming with friends near our home in La Jolla and had dived into the ocean and struck his head against a rock hidden just beneath the surface. Phyllis told me quietly, calmly that he had been permanently paralyzed from the neck down but was as smart and witty as ever and couldn't wait to see his dad. Finally, after talking briefly to my daughters and learning some happy news about my grandson, I hung up and tried to sleep.

My mind went back to George Air Force Base, Victorville, California. John was only two years old when we were stationed there. One hot summer afternoon I went with him to an ice-cream truck; we bought a half-dozen frozen popsicles. He ran excitedly in front of me back into the house. We had a powerful air cooler that kicked up quite a suction draft. As Johnny went through the door, the suction slammed it shut on his hand. I dropped those popsicles, yanked open the door, and wrapped his finger, dangling by a thread of skin, in the palm of my hand. Phyllis drove us to the emergency hospital, and the surgeon spent more than an hour sewing Johnny's little finger back on his hand.

I paced the hospital waiting room, reliving that moment, seeing the door slam, hearing his cries of pain. I would gladly have given every finger on both my hands to save my son's precious little finger. When the doctors finally came in, they said we had very little chance that he would use it again. But when a child is two years old, miracles often happen, and the finger grew back. By the time he was ten, Johnny was one great Little Leaguer.

Now he lay paralyzed from the neck down. But for a miracle, John would never move again. That night in Clark I would gladly have taken the next flight back to Hanoi and locked myself in Heartbreak if it would have given Johnny the use of his arms and legs. It was like being locked away again in solitary, powerless to change what desperately needed changing.

God had been so real to me in prison. This time when I prayed, there was no clear answer. I don't understand these things. I don't know why God seems to intervene so plainly in one event and seems so absent in another. But I refuse to let my questions overpower my faith in Him. To not believe there is a God at work in the world is a grim and unacceptable option. I do believe God is working in John's life just as he is working in mine. He has a plan for both of us. Now, John and I would have to find it together.

I don't think I slept that night. The next morning a young hospital orderly passed me the third note from one of the nurses saying she would like an interview. Security at Clark was at a maximum. We ex-POWs had determined among ourselves not to speak of prison life or conditions to anyone until all the other men were free. But this note was accompanied by a scribbled sentence from the orderly: YOU'D BETTER SEE HER, SIR. SHE'S VERY PRETTY.

So, curious, I asked the orderly to bring the nurse to the waiting room on my floor. I'll not forget that meeting. The orderly was right. Miss Ronalyn Thompson was very pretty. She also had a gift for me. It was an aluminum bracelet with my name, rank, and the date of my captivity printed on it. I'll never forget what she said when she gave me my bracelet that afternoon.

"Captain Rutledge, for many months I've worn your bracelet, without taking it off night or day. Every day I've prayed for your safe return. Now these prayers are answered. I just wanted to tell you how glad I am you're home again." Then she was gone. Later I learned that millions of Americans, young and old, from all walks of life, had been wearing ID bracelets like this one to keep the memories of the POW and MIA men clear in the public's mind and to remind them daily to pray for our safe return. I believe those prayers had everything to do with my return and, again, I am grateful.

The last leg of that journey home began February 15 as our giant transport flew towards San Diego and reunion with the ones we loved. There was so much I wanted to tell my family. There was even more I wanted to hear from them. In prison I had plenty of time to decide on the things I wanted to change in my life.

I had gone away a church dropout. I was returning transformed by what I'd seen God do in prison. I was sure that Phyllis would be happy but skeptical. In the past I hadn't even gone with her to church. Now, I wanted to be a real Christian husband and father to my family. On the plane I rehearsed what I would say.

First, I would tell her of my resolution made that torturous night in the Outhouse, when I promised God that the first Sunday of my return to freedom I would take my family to their home church. At the close of the service I would walk to the front, confess my faith in Christ, and take my responsible place as a member there with my family. In prison I had learned what it means to be isolated, struggling to build my faith alone. I had resolved never to be outside the community of Christian believers again.

Second, I had heard Colonel Flynn in a meditation at Cell 8 in Camp Unity talk about the Scripture, "Let not the sun go down upon your wrath" (Ephesians 4:26). He told how he and his wife Mary Margaret had determined in their marriage never to go to bed before an argument had been settled, the apology made, the angry words forgiven. That brief passage from God's Word really made sense to me, for often I had lain awake at night too proud to say, "I'm sorry," and both of us could feel the hurt.

That first New Year's Eve in Heartbreak Hotel I had resolved never to be without a Bible again. Those verses of God's Word that I had memorized or that I had scrounged from other prisoners' memories had been a living source of strength in my life. I was determined to begin applying God's Word in our family's life together, even in the smallest things.

Third, I can't remember ever praying with Phyllis during our entire married life. In fact, the more involved I got in my career and she in our family, the less we ever really talked with each other, let alone with God. This had to change and change fast. In prison I had worked months trying to get another man "on the line," communicating. Now I had to get my wife and family "on the line" with me. Prayer seemed the perfect way to start. So I resolved to end each day with Phyllis, talking over the day's activities and thanking God for the love we felt from each other and from Him.

Frankly, I was unsure what my wife's reaction to these resolutions might be. I determined on that long flight home to tell her the moment I landed, before we got caught up in the whirl of being together again and before my nervous pride drove me into silence.

On that plane to San Diego, flying across the Pacific Ocean, I practiced every move I would make during our reunion. This wasn't the first time we would be dramatically reunited. Phyllis was a good navy wife. We had spent much of our lifetime waiting to see each other after long tours of duty aboard a carrier or in a foreign base. No matter where I left her, she was always there waiting for me when I returned. When I would walk across the pier or runway to greet her, every reunion was the same. She would come roaring out of the crowd to embrace me in a kind of feet-off-the-ground, full-body tackle.

This time I wanted it to be different. I wanted to hold her at arm's length for one long moment, look into her eyes, tell her that I love her—and then let her tackle me. I had plans, too, for that first moment with my family. During the flight I would ask the stewardess to lend me six napkins. I was going to step off the plane, kiss Phyllis, and then hand each person in my family a napkin to kneel on. Then and there we would thank God for uniting us again. On the runway we would end this drought of prayer in our family once and for all. I had no idea that the television camera would be on us every step of the way, that all my family but Phyllis would await my arrival in the privacy of the beautiful hospital suite, or that there we would say our prayer of thanks together!

We fastened our seat belts for our final descent. The wheels touched the runway. There was a band playing, and cameras were everywhere. It seems like yesterday. I walked down the steps, saluted Admiral Joe Williams and the colors, and heard the crowd's welcome-home applause. Then out of the crowd she ran and planted her own full-body tackle on me. Her feet left the ground and almost knocked me over. All my plans to hold her at arm's length for one long moment, to tell her that I loved her, were forgotten. Thank God! Things were back to normal for the Rutledge family, but they would *never* be the same.

Part II
Phyllis Rutledge
1965-1973

II

Missing in Action

Sunday morning, November 28, 1965, my four young children and I worshiped together in the Clairemont First Southern Baptist Church of San Diego. No one remembers what happened in the service that day, but we had been inspired by the music and by the Reverend Charles W. Foley's sermon. We stopped at a supermarket nearby to pick up groceries. The children unloaded the trunk and were already in the house when our friends Jack Snyder and Merle Gorder drove into the driveway beside me. I didn't think anything strange about their visit until I saw the navy chaplain getting out of the back seat and walking toward me. Then I knew instantly. Howard was dead!

"No, no, no," I said, over and over, denying what I feared the most. I didn't faint, but my knees did give way. Immediately Merle had his arm around me, guiding me towards the house.

My tears began to flow. I wanted to be brave, a stoic navy wife, a Christian saint, but the tears came anyway. For a while there seemed to be no end of crying. As we walked in the back door, Merle was trying to comfort me.

"No, it's not that bad, Phyllis. We think he's all right. His wingman saw a chute before the plane exploded."

Inside the back door my oldest daughter Sondra, fifteen,

approached and put her arm around me. The look in her face
told me that she knew. There was no need to explain. My tears
kept falling. I wanted to stop and gather the family around. I
wanted to explain calmly and quietly that Daddy had been shot
down and was missing in action, but no words came. The older
children knew without being told. John, twelve, disappeared
immediately into his bedroom, and Peggy, seven, and Barbara,
six, were too young to really understand.

Soon, Merle's wife Kay and Jennie Speer, another family friend,
dropped by. Within minutes it seemed the house was filled with
people. Pastor Foley was there and folks from the church, navy
friends and neighbors. Their eyes were wet, their faces reflected
how deeply they shared our anguish.

As if walking in a daze, I found myself fixing refreshments,
making coffee and hopeful conversation with my friends and
neighbors. I was in a state of shock, answering the door, putting
flowers into vases, thanking people for their concern, and somehow carrying on.

I was too busy to notice that John had not come out of his
room. He was all alone in there and really suffering. Until the
last few years, John had felt his dad had always favored the
girls in our family. Recently, through their common interest in
Little League, John and his dad had become good friends. Now,
his father was missing in action. In my preoccupation with the
house filled with company, I never went near his bedroom door,
and still, today, deeply regret letting him face his sadness alone.

The crowd of friends, the noisy kitchen, the little girls playing
at my feet made it seem almost like any other day. Then the
sun went down. My body began to ache with tiredness but my
dear, thoughtful friends just would not go away. I wanted
desperately to be alone, to have a moment by myself to think it
through. Then, at last they were gone. The kids were asleep. I
walked into our bedroom and slumped down on the bed.

The first thing I noticed was Howard's picture smiling down

on me. I took the picture off the wall and held it close asking all those endless questions countless military wives have always asked.

Is he alive? Is he lying wounded somewhere in the jungle? Was he captured, even executed, or is he locked up already in an enemy prison somewhere? Will he survive?

Looking into the dark brown eyes on that photograph, I knew Howard was in the hands of God. There was nothing I could do about him but hope and pray. The real question to face now was how could we survive? In the rooms nearby were four young children who needed a father's love and attention. In the bedroom file were piles of papers, insurance policies, wills and records I could not begin to understand. In my kitchen desk were all the bills accumulating in his absence that he could straighten out in one long frantic evening when he returned. But now he wasn't coming back. I had to face those problems alone.

Being alone was nothing new. The career military wife spends a large part of her life alone. When Sondra was born, Howard was practicing jet landings on a carrier somewhere in the Pacific. When John was born, Howard was standing watch for a good friend whose basement had been flooded. When Peggy was born, my husband was stationed on a ship deployed in the Mediterranean. I've spent half my life—or so it seemed that night—waiting for him to come home and straighten out the messes I had made. Now, I didn't have a husband to take care of me or my messes. This time he wasn't coming home.

12

Despair

The morning after we learned that Howard had been shot down over North Vietnam we all made brave attempts to go on living. I fixed the children breakfast and sent them to school. I put on the coffeepot, sat down to read the morning paper, and the headlines shouted out the news again.

LOCAL NAVY PILOT—MISSING IN ACTION

For the third time in less than twenty-four hours, I was crying. To be honest, I wasn't crying only for Howard. I was also crying for Howard's wife—me. I felt lonely and deserted and afraid I couldn't handle those next long days ahead.

Then I remembered the night only eight weeks before when Howard sat me down on our bed, took out a household ledger from his briefcase and a whole notebook of instructions. Patiently, he told me how to pay bills, insurance premiums, car payments, and the like. It probably sounds silly, but this was one of the most beautiful nights of our marriage, sitting on our bed at midnight with papers spread in all directions, talking business. For the first time in our life together, he had really sat down to share all these things with me.

Maybe he had a premonition. His squadron had been flying

round-the-clock missions over North Vietnam. Several of his friends had been killed or captured. Three days before, his father had died and Howard had been forced to think of death and those whom death left behind. Apparently, Howard was trying to prepare me.

The next morning he flew to Travis Air Force Base and took a trans-Pacific flight to catch his ship. Now he was gone, and I had the ledger.

It's hard to be the head of a household with no real preparation. I started dating Howard when I was just fourteen, and he was a senior in high school. Dependence set in early. He made almost all the decisions. Even when he was stationed on a ship halfway round the world, I knew I could call him or write a letter and ask how to handle this or settle that. Now he couldn't tell me what to do.

Fortunately, in the days and months ahead, there was little time to waste regretting. The children were growing up fast, and I had to be both mom and dad to all of them. Sondra was a teen-ager with boyfriends and dates to think about. Helping her through those awkward teen-age years was an awesome responsibility. I've always been too easygoing. Howard had always disciplined the children. He made the rules. He enforced them. Now with Howard gone, it was my task to get my daughters through. Fortunately, I had been a teen-age girl once and had some experience to fall back on.

Raising John was something else. He was a wonderful boy, and like his father he was full of energy and strong-willed. He was often in trouble for his temper. John was lonely and angry. He missed his father very much and needed a man in his life.

I knew how he felt. I needed a man in my life, too. But Howard was not dead. He was missing. So, I was not a wife. I was not a widow. I was nothing. I still loved Howard and never thought once of ending our marriage. So John, Sondra, the little girls, and their unhappy mother would just have to wait and see what happened next.

I got really despondent during those first two years. I would pray and pray and nothing would happen. Often I would ask God, "Just let me have anything to know that Howard is alive and that all of this suffering is good for something." It seemed my prayers went unanswered.

There were some little answers we clung to along the way, hoping that God had heard our prayers. For example, my mother-in-law received an envelope with a foreign tea bag inside. It was addressed to Howard's dad who had passed away just before Howard had been shot down. We wondered if someone was trying to send us a message. I knew if Howard were trying to communicate in code, it might possibly be from the Bible. So, scratching at straws, I looked up *tea* in our Bible concordance. I found one Scripture in the Book of Haggai. The verse included such lines as "I have just enough to eat to keep from being hungry. I have just enough clothing to keep from being cold." That fit our idea of prison perfectly so our hopes soared. Then I realized that Howard hadn't read the Bible in years. Surely he wouldn't begin using it with a passage from an obscure Old Testament book like Haggai!

Finally, we sent the bag to navy authorities who reported back that some crackpot was sending them around indiscriminately to other families.

I was really desperate. It seemed that God had abandoned us. Our church attendance and our spirits fell.

Howard and I were both reared in loyal Southern Baptist households. In our homes, as children, it was family tradition to attend church every time the church doors opened. We would go to Sunday school faithfully and stay for morning worship. Sunday nights the family would all go back for choir practice and Baptist Training Union. On Wednesday nights we went to

Bible study and prayer meeting, while Thursday nights we often joined the evangelism visitation teams.

But something happened when Howard and I got married. Stationed at Pensacola, Howard only went to church three or four times and then dropped out completely. Every time I asked him to join us at church, he would answer, "Not today, Honey. I'm too tired," or "I think I'll just stay at home and read the paper," or "There's a ball game on TV, and it's my only chance to relax and see one."

He was never sarcastic, nor did he try to get me to stop going. He just lost interest himself. Howard's career was really climbing. He said he couldn't be active in church the way he should be and still be a good fighter pilot. He got active in the happy-hour cocktail circuit on Friday nights and eventually threw off all the constraints his parents had enforced during those teenage years.

We never had liquor in our homes as children. We never went to shows on Sundays, never even played cards, and any kind of swearing was rewarded with a mouthful of soap or a switching. Now, Howard was boss in his own family, and he rebelled against his strict Oklahoma Baptist background.

By the time we had children, the only services Howard would attend were the memorial services for his friends lost in battle.

For a while, in Jacksonville, I had a friend whose pilot husband also was losing interest in the church. We would plot and scheme to get our husbands there. Every Sunday morning I would look around the congregation to see if she had her husband in tow. She would give the A-OK sign if her husband was there or look discouraged and shake her head if he wasn't. It was kind of comical at first. Eventually, we both quit trying.

I was worried what his not attending church would do to our children. When Sundays came around and I went through the house saying, "Get up, it's time for Sunday school," I was answered by a series of groans. "Daddy's not going; why should we go?" After Howard disappeared, I grew more and more depressed. Feeling pity for myself, it was easier just to stay in bed on Sundays. Eventually I dropped out of church, too.

One afternoon two years after Howard was shot down, I was visiting my mother when she became very ill. She had had a stroke; and only days after the operation to save her, she died. During her funeral I cried tears of guilt for all those things I should have done. I should have written more; I should have called more. I loved my mother, but in my preoccupation with survival, I had seldom even seen her in the past few years. Now I felt guilty and even more alone. First Howard is shot down—now this! What tragedy would strike us next?

The third tragic blow fell on July 4, 1968. School was out. The children were restless. The house was full of John's and Sondra's teen-age friends. I had planned on sending John to Oklahoma to spend the summer with my sister and her son, but she beat me to the punch and sent her boy to spend the summer with me. We planned a July 4 picnic at the beach. The summer before, at a similar picnic in Tulsa, my sister had been injured in the head by a firework tossed from a crowd, so we tried to find a quiet beach away from holiday dangers.

John was like a fish in the ocean. He and his visiting cousin, Mark, loved to see which one could hold his breath the longest under water. They were diving and swimming and having a great time. On one particular dive John stayed under far too long. Suddenly, I could see a black boy pulling a white boy through the surf, one arm around his waist and the other around his neck. It was John, and it looked as if he had drowned. I ran to his side in panic. Apparently, he had dived into the water and struck his head on a rock beneath the surface. The stranger saved my boy from drowning. I never even had the opportunity to thank him.

We called an ambulance and rushed John to the emergency

hospital. The first person I thought to call was Pastor Foley. He came immediately. An outstanding young neurosurgeon happened to be on the staff of that hospital and recommended immediate surgery. Brother Foley had been a medic in World War II. He explained the options and after he prayed, I decided to permit the operation. Then we waited. During those endless hours, I prayed. It was the first time I had prayed in months, but I prayed hard. "Don't let John die!" It seemed the past few years I had had to watch all my family suffer. I felt so helpless. I wanted to bear their pain, but all that I could do was stand helplessly by.

Finally, the surgeons walked out of the operating room and sat down beside me. I could tell their news was bad news.

"Mrs. Rutledge, your son is paralyzed from the neck down. He is alive but will probably never move again."

John was only fifteen years old. He was just becoming a man. He had so much life ahead of him, and now he was paralyzed. How much grief were we to bear? Where was God in all this? Was He punishing us for something I had or hadn't done? Was He testing me?

Brother Foley talked softly of a God who stood helplessly by as His own Son, Jesus, died on a Roman cross. With tears in his eyes, Pastor Foley talked about a heavenly Father who understood our pain and shared our sorrow. We can't understand the mystery of suffering. But we can know that God has promised never to leave us or forsake us. The words poured out, and somehow I got hold of hope. I didn't understand the tragedy that struck my son that day. I felt guilty and responsible, but I prayed for strength, and God heard my prayer.

13

Hope

For the next few months after John's accident, I went overboard trying to help him. He lay helplessly on his bed, needing total care day and night. I worked around the clock to make him feel comfortable and entertained. If he called, I was there. After all, he was only fifteen years old and needed all the attention I could give him. Besides, I was feeling more and more responsible for the accident. Often, while feeding or bathing my son, I asked myself hard and useless questions. Could the accident have been avoided? If I had been more careful, would John be well today? Will his father think I failed him, that his son is crippled because of my neglect?

The guilty feelings multiplied as I grew tense and overworked. Peggy and Barbara needed more of my time. Sondra was going steady and also needed attention. I was working day and night and gradually falling apart. I knew something had to change as my own frustration mounted to a dangerous level.

All during this time, Pastor Foley and the people of Clairemont First Southern Baptist Church were praying. During the seven years of imprisonment, our family was mentioned in public prayer every Sunday morning faithfully. There were cards and calls of encouragement, cookies and candy for John. I wasn't attending church, but Pastor Foley and his wife still visited often. They didn't berate or badger me. On every visit they would chat a while, share words of encouragement, and say a brief prayer. Then, usually on the way to the door, Brother Foley would invite us to church on Sunday. I never felt pressured. Somehow I knew he understood. Even if we didn't attend, the people at First Church never gave up on us. They were faithful when I wasn't, just as God is faithful when we aren't.

It was my two young ones, Peggy and Barbara, who got me going back to church. They became very active in the youth group and loved singing in the choir. Their enthusiasm was contagious. I went to church when I could be sure John was well taken care of, and, the house cleaned, the dishes done, the bills paid, the records kept, the girls ready, and myself presentable. I was trying to do everything and ended up getting more and more irritable with John, impatient with the girls, and angry at myself.

The tension of not hearing anything about my husband for five long years was getting to me. I still didn't know if he were alive or dead. I was trying to be both mom and dad to my growing brood; eventually, I realized that unless something happened I couldn't keep it all together. For a while we had an attendant for John. When he left and my health failed, I had to put John in a nursing home where he could get professional care.

I have to admit that I wasn't aware that God was working in my life during those first years of waiting. But as I look back, it is plain to see that God was working, even then. He was working through people who cared enough to reach out and lift us up. Howard's mother was really used by God to help us survive. She visited us from Tulsa and helped clean up the house, fixed roasts and stews and chocolate pies. She would talk with John and play with the girls. At night, when we couldn't sleep, she would pray and quote promises of hope from the Bible. Before John's accident, she had been the one who noticed him crying during an invitation at church and together they went forward to pray and commit John's life to Christ. He was only eleven, but he and his grandma did important spiritual business that day. No one makes mother-in-law jokes around me anymore. I've seen what a god-send a mother-in-law can be.

LaVerne Barger, one of my Sunday-school teachers at First Church, was another important friend God used. She always seemed to know when I needed her. Invariably she would appear at our door with food or flowers or books just when I was getting low. She and the pastor often visited John and talked with him about the Bible and baseball. Brother Foley once told me that John could ask deeper questions about the Bible than any boy his age. It was good to see my son take an interest in God's Word.

Ken Masat, Howard's wingman who saw his chute that day, also visited John and talked enthusiastically about airplanes and flying. Ken is a Catholic, and I was pleased to learn from him one day that his church, too, was praying for us.

Other people helped. The city of Bellflower, California, adopted Howard as their prisoner of war and sent the family gifts and gave John a thousand-dollar scholarship.

God was using all kinds of people to help fill the emptiness in our lives, but nothing could really satisfy until we heard from Howard.

About Thanksgiving 1970 I went to my mailbox and pulled out a handful of bills and fourth-class ads. There was a POW folder and like all the other folders I had gotten I supposed it contained news reprints and important speeches about the prisoners or the war. Usually I just opened these folders, skimmed their contents, and tossed them in the trash. This time a strange-looking letter fell out. There were Vietnamese words printed on the cover and inside in a square there were seven beautiful handwritten lines from Howard.

I screamed with delight and ran into the house yelling at the top of my voice, "He's alive. Your daddy is alive." Of course, our joy was tempered slightly by his words "very minor injury." Was he

A reproduction of the first letter Phyllis Rutledge received from her husband—five years after he was captured.

just hiding the truth from us, or was he really well? But the handwriting was obviously his. He was alive for sure. After five years of being suspended between hope and despair, hope tipped the scales.

That Thanksgiving Sunday my family and I took the letter to church and Pastor Foley read it from the pulpit. When he finished reading those seven short lines, he bowed his head and said a prayer of thanks. I will always remember that Thanksgiving and the gratitude I felt to God and to this pastor and his people for the love they had shown to me and my family.

In the next two years there were only a dozen or so other letters from Howard, but it was easy to read between the lines. My husband's Christian life was growing. He had shown almost no spiritual leadership in our home in the past twenty years, but it sounded as if something had happened to him to change all that. It got me thinking about my own spiritual growth. I began to read the Bible. I read books on prayer, and I began to pray again. The family went to church regularly and found our real friends were there. People like Virginia Smith and Yvonne Boling were quick to help out in a crisis and never expected to be thanked for their thoughtfulness. I don't know what I would have done without the people at First Church.

Meanwhile, John was really losing ground in the nursing home. Surrounded by old people who were dying, constantly aware of the sadness and despair around him, John's morale was sinking fast. One afternoon I walked out of the nursing home knowing that if I didn't get him out of there soon, we would lose our son. I was afraid he might get on drugs or even try suicide. He had every reason to be depressed. But I had no idea where to take him.

The next morning I decided something must be done. In Sunday-school class one of my friends had told of a recent experience when she and her family "let Jesus take them out to dinner." It may sound farfetched, but they got into their car and asked God to lead them to a restaurant. They drove through the streets of La Jolla, turning down one street and up another. Then they felt it was time to stop. There was a restaurant nearby that they had never tried. So they went in, had a wonderful evening, a delicious meal, paid the bill, and thanked God for His guidance.

So I thought to myself, "What can I lose?" If God cares about dinner, surely He cares about my son's suffering! I'll try trusting God to lead me to a place that can help John. So I got up, got dressed, climbed into the car, and prayed for guidance. There was a new rehabilitation center nearby and it seemed natural to start there. So, I drove towards Clairemont Mesa Boulevard and Sharps Hospital. I got out of the car, walked into the brand-new reception area, and to my surprise found John's doctor in the corridor as if waiting for me. I don't know about your experience trying to catch a doctor in, but this was something new for me.

I walked up to Dr. A. J. Russell and said, "I have to talk with you."

Surprised, he answered, "Fine!" We sat down on a bench, and I told him my fears about John's living in that place, surrounded by death and the dying, growing more and more depressed.

He answered with concern. "I've just been talking with some old med-school friends of mine who are starting an experimental rehabilitation center for young people in Tempe, Arizona. I'll call them about John, and we'll see what they can do." I mumbled words of thanks and made a hasty retreat from the hospital.

I don't pretend my faith was strong. I didn't even know for sure he would call me back. But he did, and not long after, John was flown to Tempe, Arizona, and the Good Samaritan Rehabilitation Center. It was a miracle, and it came just in time. And though he is still paralyzed, today he is studying at University of California at Berkeley.

Thanks to God and all the people who cared, we were making headway. I even got the checkbook balanced now and then. But the big question remained. When would the war end so that Howard could come home?

POW AND MIA wives around the country were beginning to feel that it might never end. We organized our small informal groups into a national organization and worked to keep the prisoners' plight before the public. It's easy to forget a man when he has been in prison seven years. We could not let the public forget.

The National League of Families of POW and MIA in Southeast Asia worked hard writing congressmen, the military, and the press. Other groups sold bracelets with the prisoner's name, rank, and date of capture to raise money to help our cause and, again, to keep our men remembered. Thousands of people wore those bracelets. Hundreds of them wrote me that they were praying for Howard and for his safe return.

As the talks in Paris continued and Dr. Henry Kissinger dashed around the world, we held our breath and prayed for our president. He was only human and had a superhuman task to perform. Like all of us, he would make mistakes, but he tried, as we were trying, to get our men home again.

One Christmas would come and go, and we would say, "Next Christmas they'll be home." Then another twelve months would slowly pass with no real hope in sight. I tried to be casual about the whole thing, but my excitement mounted as the talks in Paris and the secret visits to Peking, Moscow, and Hanoi were made known. Then, unbelievably, the peace was signed. Sunday, January 28, 1973, early in the morning we got a call— Howard was coming home!

14

Reunion

After learning from Operation Homecoming that Howard would soon be released, I rushed down to the church, told Pastor Foley that this would be our day, and then rushed home to await further news. Again, the church service stopped and the people thanked God together for answer to prayer. Every time the phone rang, I thought I'd faint with excitement. First, it was Howard's mom calling from Tulsa. She had just hung up, disappointed that there had been no more news, when the phone rang again. The navy was calling to officially notify me that Howard was to be included in the first group coming out of Hanoi.

I didn't let myself get too excited. He wasn't free yet. All we had been told was that he would be flown to Clark Air Force Base in the Philippines. We were also told that there would be no press there, but that we would be sent a picture immediately when he arrived.

Two weeks passed. They were the longest weeks of my life. Would Howard be the same? How had prison changed him? Would he be well? How would he react when I told him of John's accident and paralysis? Would he blame me? Would he approve of the new house I had bought and of the way I had managed the ledger he gave me seven years ago?

Then my phone rang again. An excited neighbor reported the first plane was landing at Clark. The girls ran to the television, and together we watched the first load of men climb down. No Howard. Our phone was ringing off the hook. The people at First Church had been praying seven years, and they really got involved in their praying. Now in homes all over the neighborhood, they were waiting to see the man they had been praying for. We were all going crazy with excitement by the time the second plane landed.

Thirty-nine men got off, one by one they said their words of thanks, saluted the military officers, then walked the long red carpet to freedom. Still no Howard. Then a slender, black-haired man climbed off the plane. The newsman's voice grew silent. Then we heard him say, with a kind of laugh, "Captain Howard Rutledge; he says his name is Howie."

A cheer that God couldn't help but hear went up that day from the Rutledge house and from the houses of the people of First Church. A thousand voices hoarse with hollering, two thousand hands back-slapping, and a thousand people dancing with joy around their living rooms! Howard's home! I'm sure that God knew that those cheers were our way of saying thanks for bringing Howard home.

The cameras were close. We all saw him clearly. He looked thin, but he was walking, head high; and when he saluted Admiral Gayler, we could tell he was all right. He called me three times from the Philippines during the next three days. Each time it was about 3 A.M., I think. He talked very low and very slowly. And the conversations were a bit strained. You know how it is when you've been storing up things to say for years, and then when it's time to say them, you freeze with excitement.

When I finally had the courage to tell him about John, he

paused for one long moment. Then he spoke. "Phyllis, do you blame yourself for Johnny's accident?" I mumbled something tearfully; then slowly, calmly, as though we were back on that bed the midnight I had seen him last, he said, "Phyllis, I trust you in all things. I know you did your very best. That's all anyone can ask."

I learned a lot about God that day. Howard's voice went on, "We can do all things through Christ which strengtheneth us" (*see* Philippians 4:13).

The day Howard was due home in San Diego, the doorbell rang, and a deliveryman handed me a beautiful orchid. It was from my husband. Not since high school had he sent me orchids. Then the government limousine arrived to take us down to Miramar.

It was a dreary, rainy day. I wondered on that short drive to the airport why the sun wasn't shining and the birds singing for Howard's return. The weather got worse as we approached the airport. Imagine San Diego with hail so heavy that it left the golf course looking as if it were covered with snow!

When we arrived at the operations building at Miramar there were TV and radio reporters, cameras, microphones, and mobs of excited people. The plane was due any minute. We were told to wait for our husbands in our limousine, but when I saw another wife standing on the field, I jumped out and ran across the VIP area to get a closer look. Other wives saw me and followed. Suddenly, the sun broke through the clouds, and the silver plane bearing my husband landed and taxied to the waiting crowd. One by one the men got down, and then, as if in a dream, he was standing there. How often I had seen him across crowded waiting rooms, piers, and runways! How often my heart had skipped a beat as he smiled and held out his arms in greeting. But he had been gone so long. Would he smile? Would he hold out his arms again?

Then I heard his name. "Captain Howard Rutledge!" I waited. He saluted Admiral Williams, greeted the press, looked into the crowd. Our eyes met. He smiled and held out his arms. I ran and felt his embrace, my heart crying out its thanks to the God who brought us back together again.

Faith in God Sustained Him, Ex-POW Tells Congregation

BY HAROLD KEEN .
Times Staff Writer

SAN DIEGO—A Navy flier imprisoned more than seven years in Vietnam went to church Sunday to thank those who had prayed for his freedom.

Capt. Howard Rutledge came home Thursday and was released from a Navy hospital—as were 10 of 15 ex-prisoners in San Diego—to spend the weekend as he wished. Some of the men went for drives or visits. Some went shopping.

Rutledge went to church.

Word had spread that he would be at the First Southern Baptist Church of Clairemont and there was a crowd of 700 filling the church for the late morning worship service when he arrived.

Rutledge, 44, wore his khaki uniform. His mother, his wife, his two teen-age daughters, and his married daughter and his grandson accompanied him. His family belongs to the church, but Rutledge left for Asia before he could have his membership transferred here.

The pastor, the Rev. Charles W. Foley Jr., asked Rutledge to speak to the congregation. He was given an ovation which lasted almost five minutes. He stood in front of the congregation and told the crowd:

"I was able to sustain life and hope through the faith I have in God. I am here today also because of the prayers of Christian people while I was in prison."

He urged everyone to place their trust in God—because, he said, there was no other place to put it. He thanked the congregation for its prayers on his behalf.

Please Turn to Page 20, Col. 1

FAITH IN GOD

Continued from First Page

He officially joined the church at the Sunday service. He had been a member of another Southern Baptist congregation before being transferred to San Diego.

Mr. Foley said that five others in the audience, moved by the captain's testimonial, "were inspired to accept the Lord."

Afterward, Rutledge gathered with members of his family at the home in the University City district which his wife had bought in his absence. He had not seen his grandson —the 3-year-old son of his oldest daughter, Sondra Tollison—before his return from Vietnam.

Rutledge was one of the former prisoners who got what the Navy called an "open gangway" for the weekend after passing preliminary medical examinations.